THE
HEART
of PRAISE

JACK HAYFORD

THE HEART of PRAISE

Daily Ways to Worship the Father with Psalms

Regal Books
A Division of Gospel Light
Ventura, California, U.S.A.

Published by Regal Books
A Division of Gospel Light
Ventura, California U.S.A.
Printed in U.S.A.

Library of Congress Cataloging-in-Publication Data
Hayford, Jack W.
     The heart of praise : daily ways to praise the Father with Psalms / Jack W.
Hayford.
     ISBN 0-8307-1609-2
     1. Bible. O.T. Psalms—Meditations. 2. Devotional calendars.
I. Title.
BS1430.4.H395 1992
242'.2—dc20
                                                                    92-23577
                                                                         CIP

4 5 6 7 8 9 10 / KP / X3.1 / 99 98 97 96 95 94

Rights for publishing this book in other languages are contracted by Gospel
Literature International (GLINT). GLINT also provides technical help for the
adaptation, translation, and publishing of Bible study resources and books in
scores of languages worldwide. For further information, contact GLINT, Post
Office Box 488, Rosemead, California, 91770, U.S.A., or the publisher.

Table of Contents

As We Begin, Together...

Dear friend, I am hopeful—no, I'm persuaded!—that the praise and worship you offer our heavenly Father through the Psalms in this little book can bless you beyond anything you might expect! You do know, don't you? *God wants to bless you through worship.* He deserves our praise, of course. But He also delights in it, and for a reason. He calls for our praise, not because He needs a "build up," but because this atmosphere provides Him with a mighty opportunity for Him to bless us!!

There is nothing egocentric about worshiping with that awareness in our minds. It's not a matter of our cheapening worship, seeking only to win a blessing. It's simply that our being blessed has been "built in" to worship as an inherent by-product in the practice of praise. God has ordained that praise and worship ascend like arrows, puncturing the heavens and allowing His abundant riches to rain down.

A word of caution: Praising God through the Psalms will change you. The change will be a glorious one, but since all change is threatening to some, I wanted to warn you. The fact is, worship *changes us into the likeness of the one we worship.* In speaking of the worship of idols the psalmist said, "Those who make them are like them; so is everyone who trusts in them" (Ps. 115:8). Worship has the awesome power to transform the worshiper into the image of the one worshiped. If you or I worship the god of mammon or materialism, we will become more materialistic—more ruled by the world-mind. Similarly, worshiping the god of unbridled sensuousness has reduced many a devotee of the flesh to a fleshly degenerate. But in contrast, worshiping the true and living God "in the beauty of holiness" will in turn make you and me more "beautiful" people—truly! Praising the God of grace will make us more gracious. We'll prove the truth of the saying, "As He is, so are we in this world" (1 John 4:17).

And there is no greater pathway to praise than the Psalms. With this ancient Jewish hymnbook as the basis for our praise, we *breathe in* God's own Word while *breathing out* our worship of Him. The Psalms fairly burst with praise and adoration that glorifies God for who He is, while at the same time showing us who we are. In the Psalms we are reminded that worship is a way of telling us something about ourselves, more than a ritual of reminding God of how great He is, as though He has a low self-image and needs us to encourage Him to think better of Himself. We can learn truths about ourselves while standing with hands upraised, or kneeling, or lying prostrate before the throne that we can learn in no other position.

Since so many of the Psalms were written by David, this book will also expose you to the very soul of a man who was "after [God's] own heart" (1 Sam. 13:14). In the Psalms, David and other inspired writers bring us to the heart of the kind of worship God wants. And the heart of worship is declaring "worth-ship"—God's worth and wonder. Both in his joy and in his pain, David declares God's worthiness; reminding us that praise and worship belong both in our moments of triumph and exultation, and at life's painful extremities. As someone has said, "faith can be born in a cry."

The guidelines for praise that follow have been arranged topically for convenient, private use in your daily devotions, or for special times of fellowship with your family or other fellow believers. For the Psalms not only lend themselves to individual worship, but they also highlight the importance of "not forsaking the assembling of ourselves together" (Heb. 10:25). As you allow me to share my thoughts with you, I believe you'll profit from the excellent work Ron Durham has done in providing stimulating questions and thought-provokers, designed to massage the truths I've shared into practical application. The added Scripture references are his selections, and prompt my thanks to him and his devoted work in outlining this whole project. Incidentally, there are also some suggestions in the Appendix you might find helpful for structuring your private times of prayer and praise.

So open your heart with me. Let's both come to Him in worship! Worship is *the* pathway, the grand entry gate, for welcoming the King of heaven into our daily lives, our families, our churches, our cities, our nation. May your use of these reflections make a straight path for His feet...and for yours.

Jack Hayford

1
The Call to Worship

"Oh come, let us worship and bow down; let us kneel before the Lord our Maker. For He is our God, and we are the people of His pasture, and the sheep of His hand."—Psalm 95:6,7

I confess to being old enough to remember the then famous Don McNeil "Breakfast Club" on radio. The program came out of Chicago, and was something of the equivalent of television's "Today" show now. Though I was only a boy, how well I recall how during each day's program there would be a time when Don would say, "It's prayer time around the breakfast table." Soft organ music would rise in the background, then Don would continue: "And now, each in his own words, each in his own way, bow your heads and let us pray." It's moving to recollect such a thing being included on a nationwide, secular program!

And yet there was something about the "Breakfast Club's" invitation to worship that was much more "American" than it was scriptural. We have a national disposition to emphasize our right to worship "in our own way." While I'm grateful for that freedom, of course, it misses an essential fact about true worship: biblical worship is on *God's* terms, not ours. Psalm 95, in calling us to worship, says nothing about our rights. Instead, it summarily calls us to *bow down*, to *kneel* before this One before whose creatures we are, sheep of His pasture. And make no mistake—the call to bowing and kneeling is more than merely to bodily postures. It focuses the surrender of our will and way to Him. It means that we are granting supreme authority to God; that in worship and in life we are giving up our will in favor of His. It notes a foundational fact about true worship: Once I choose the Living God as my God, *I give up the right to worship "in my own way."* In the very act of naming God *God*, you and I are granting to Him alone the right to prescribe how He wishes to be worshiped.

For example, in Genesis 22 when God told Abraham to go to the land of Moriah *to worship*, we're introduced to God's ways in appointing the "worship program" for those He plans to grow up in faith's ways. Abraham had no occasion to say, "Sure, God! I *will* worship You—but how about in my own way, OK?" Rather, when Abraham hears God say he's to worship by offering his son Isaac on an altar of sacrifice, he knows he has to choose between his way and God's.

What a shock to hear God's appointed worship plan! Offer Isaac!? This not only apparently went against God's revealed displeasure with pagan practices of human sacrifice; but God had also actually given Isaac as a special gift to Abraham and Sarah after they were past the normal age of childbearing. And now, to demand Isaac's life? But outlandish though it seemed, Abraham is ready to obey. And he tells his servants something very significant: "The lad and I will go yonder and *worship*" (Gen. 22:5, *KJV*, emphasis mine).

Of course, today we know the story's end; how God provided another sacrifice—a ram caught in the thicket; how young Isaac's life was spared. Yet the New Testament says that Abraham "offered" Isaac, because faith's living worship was found in his obedience and willingness (Heb. 11:17). He had demonstrated the basic meaning of worship: *totally giving over my will to the will of God.*

As we begin, we are wise to expect to be *shaped* in understanding and practice as we answer God's call to worship. We'll find it not only a privilege, but a challenge. Be aware and be prepared: To grow in praise and worship is to discover new dimensions of saying to God, *Not my will but thine be done.*

Praise in Prayer

O God, I confess both the difficulty and yet the desirability of totally submitting my will to Yours. Help me as I launch forward toward new, heartfelt praise and worship. And help me to love and trust You so deeply that I am assured that whatever I give up for You will be only gain for me. In the name of Jesus, Amen.

Selected Readings

Exodus 35:20-29   Hebrews 5:5-9
Exodus 39:32-43   Hebrews 8:1-6

Praise in Practice

1. What "idols" or objects of worship do you find substituted for God today? Is pride often involved in the naming of these "gods"?

2. To bring this question closer to home, take a piece of paper, and on it draw a circle three or four inches in diameter. Write inside the circle the three or four things most dear to you, besides God and Christ (family, work, friends, etc.). Now imagine that God calls you to sacrifice everything in the circle, leaving it only for Him. What would be the hardest to put outside the circle? Would you be angry with God for requiring this? Of course God does not require you to sacrifice your family. But this exercise confronts us with the *attitude* required of true worshipers.

2
Discoveries of Praise

"Teach me Your way, O Lord; I will walk in Your truth; unite my heart to fear Your name. I will praise You, O Lord my God, with all my heart, and I will glorify Your name forevermore."—Psalm 86:11,12

People who would truly worship God must become *teachable* people. Here, the psalmist looks up to God with complete openness, ready both to learn and to walk in the truth. To unfold this theme, return to the account of Abraham's offering up Isaac. No passage in Scripture provides more fundamental teaching on the true meaning of worship.

By being open to God's call, Abraham discovered *a new place of worship.* "Go to the land of Moriah," God told him, "and offer [Isaac] there as a burnt offering on one of the mountains of which I shall tell you" (Gen. 22:2). And Abraham left the security of his caravan and his servants to go discover this new place—this new mountain of acceptable worship to God.

Sometimes we must go to a new "place," too, in

order to discover the true meaning of worship. It will probably be more a new place in our hearts or attitudes, rather than to a new physical site; but we sometimes need to be pointed away from the worn valleys of our familiar ways to a mountain of God's assignment. We can become so accustomed to tradition, to the same trappings of worship, the same forms, that the spirit of worship dies of familiarity. But let's open as the Psalmist: "Teach me *Your* way." Let's not fear discovering a new place of worship, where in finding new and fresh capacities for worship, we find new dimensions of God's goodness and Person.

Abraham first discovered that *surrendering to God's claim* is at the core of worship. Abraham thought Isaac was *his;* momentarily forgetting that Isaac was God's gift and thereby rightfully His to claim. And so it is with all of our own gifts. Everything we have has been "bought at a price" (1 Cor. 6:20); and you and I need to retain a readiness to return our "beloved Isaacs" at the center of our hearts—those things we cherish most dearly. Ever and always they must be kept before the Lord, to be sacrificed for His purpose. In the text for this reading, the psalmist promises to praise God with his whole heart, clearly meaning that nothing can be withheld. Can we begin to sense here the radical nature of true worship? It transforms our values from the beginning.

But further, Abraham discovered *the true nature of God.* He learned that God does not demand those things dearest to us because *He needs them,* but because He knows *we need* to be released from their controlling us. God never demands a sacrifice for the divine plea-

18

sure of smelling its aroma, or because He needs us to tickle His pride. The objective is our release—our growth. God asked Abraham to offer Isaac, neither to exploit Abraham's emotions or to destroy Isaac's body. But what He did do was to forever take away Abraham's fear that God might not have his best interest at heart. It is only in living worship that we will draw closely enough to discern God's true nature and loving heart toward us.

Abraham also discovered *the rewards of worship*. Of course, God gave Abraham no immediate monetary reward for worshiping Him; but the reward was immensely grander—*God Himself!* "I am your...exceedingly great reward" (Gen. 15:1). But until every corner of Abraham's heart was possessed by a trust in the greater love of God, God would be restricted from so fully giving of Himself to Abraham. There wouldn't have been room in Abraham's heart to contain the wealth awaiting him in God, if he was withholding anything from God. It's another way of saying, "No one can serve two masters" (Matt. 6:24); the sacrifice of worship establishing our servanthood to the true God.

We see, then, that worship has a "cutting edge"— one that cuts the flesh and prunes our preferences. Bowing before the Sovereign Lord introduces real demands, but also opens new dimensions of promise. We begin to catch a glimpse of what we can discover about God, and about ourselves, when we are willing to be taught in worship by Him *whom* we worship.

Praise in Prayer

Dear Lord, the extent of Your lordship over my life would be frightening if I did not trust You to have my best interests in mind. Grant me a teachable spirit, that I may discover the riches You have in store for those who put You first in their lives. Through Christ I pray, Amen.

Selected Readings

Genesis 22:1-19   Luke 18:18-30
1 Samuel 3:10-18   Hebrews 11:17,18

Praise in Practice

1. After giving careful thought to your pilgrimage in Christ, share something you have learned that may never have been revealed to you except for your accepting some discipline as a disciple of our Lord Jesus!

2. Do new worship forms, or even unfamiliar places of worship, make you uncomfortable? Why or why not?

3
The Beauty of Holiness

"Give unto the Lord, O you mighty ones, give unto the Lord glory and strength. Give unto the Lord the glory due to His name; worship the Lord in the beauty of holiness."—Psalm 29:1,2

All of us have our own ideas about what makes a worship service beautiful. The fact that we sometimes disagree on that may indicate that we might be missing a clue the psalmist gives here about worship's intent. The text points to something called "the beauty of holiness." It seems that in worship, God is wanting to meet us and pour *His* beauty and His holiness into our lives. Could it be that if our worship more frequently "beautified" us, we'd more readily find "holiness" than by self-constructed programs of religious effort?

This psalm's mention of the presence of the holy God may seem threatening to some, prompting us to recoil in unworthiness or with self-disgust rather than being attracted to God's holiness. How many of us feel all too keenly that, in comparison to the All-Holy-One, we are anything but holy! That was the prophet Isaiah's experience when he saw a vision of the Lord, "high and lifted up," with the seraphim—those mysterious creatures that surround God's throne; who ceaselessly worship God's holiness, crying, "Holy, holy, holy is the Lord of hosts; the whole earth is full of His glory!" (Isa. 6:3).

Isaiah could only cry out, "Woe is me!" (Interestingly, we can almost hear a good Jewish worshiper like Isaiah call out *"Oveh!"*—that's the Hebrew word used here for "woe.") Then the prophet adds, "For I am undone! Because I am a man of unclean lips, and I dwell in the midst of a people of unclean lips; for my eyes have seen the King, the Lord of hosts" (vs. 5).

Surely our own worship would be shallow if we could not feel, with Isaiah, something of the fearful distance between God's holiness and ours. Yet there is more to worship than this. For look!—suddenly one of the seraphim flies to the altar of sacrifice, takes a coal from it, touches the prophet's tongue with the burning coal and says: "Behold, this has touched your lips; your iniquity is taken away, and your sin purged" (vs. 7).

From one standpoint, you are exactly right if you feel that you're too sinful to stand in the presence of God and worship. But let our worship "in Christ"—in "the beauty of *His* holiness"—remind us how His cleansing blood has touched us. Not only our tongues but our whole being—"washed in the blood of the Lamb"! It *is* overwhelming to reflect on our sinfulness before a sinless God, but let us recognize with equal impact that through Christ we have been cleansed; enabled through no righteousness of our own, to stand before the holy God.

If we dare to confess that we have been stained with sin, we can also believe with equal boldness that Christ's holiness will clothe us. In the beauty of holiness—in robes of righteousness—He enables us to stand before Him, high and lifted up though He is, and our worship is fully accepted by Him! And as we worship, let's welcome the fire of God's altar to be applied directly to any point of failure which remains. As Isaiah's "unclean lips" troubled him, and were purged, believe whatever troubles you have may be similarly purged as you worship—discovering *more* of "the beauty of holiness" as it overwhelms our unholiness!

Praise in Prayer

Holy, holy, holy, Lord God Almighty! Through the blood of Christ I praise You for clothing me in His righteousness and admitting me into Your throne room to gaze on the beauty of Your holiness, Amen.

Selected Readings

Isaiah 6:1-8   Hebrews 12:18-29
Hebrews 10:19-22   Revelation 4:6-11

Praise in Practice

1. Picture or describe the most beautiful worship setting you've ever seen. Is it a cathedral? A woodland setting? A view from a mountaintop? Now compare that scene with the awesome picture painted in Isaiah 6:1-8. Dwell on that until the beauty of the other scenes fade in comparison with the beauty of God's own holiness.

2. Practice—now, and several times throughout a day or two—this twofold prayer of *confession* and *consolation:* (1) Ask God to forgive your sins in the name of Christ, then (2) affirm joyfully, *"My sins are forgiven!"* Do you find it harder to affirm forgiveness than to confess sin? If so, how might this inhibit your worship?

4
Pain and Praise and the Presence of God

> "O My God, I cry in the daytime, but You
> do not hear; and in the night season, and am
> not silent. But You are holy, who inhabit the
> praises of Israel."—Psalm 22:2,3

The Psalms, though great, swelling songs to God, can often be raw and ragged since they are so honest-to-life as well as honest-to-God. They give vent to sorrow and anguish as well as to exultation. Some people mistakenly think that life has to be going smoothly in order for them to worship. Not the psalmists. To be sure, they can shout and sing with joy. But they also know to worship when the heart is burdened with grief, and sometimes their songs are wrenched from their groanings.

They reveal that worship is appropriate in every setting and circumstance of life; that you and I can develop a capacity for praise that will allow it to break through to God quite independently of any "night seasons" we feel at any given moment.

Once when my schedule had weighed me down with an awful burden of mental and spiritual pressure, I took a break and traveled up Highway 1, curving along California's beautiful Pacific coastline. Coming to a little spot called Jade Cove, I stopped the car and walked down to the edge of the ocean. I heard the crashing of the waves, and felt their spray on my face. And there, semi-surrounded by the splashing sea, I poured out my plight in prayer, like David in Psalm 22.

Suddenly, with an inexplicable "lifting" effect, a marvelous flood of peace swept over my entire being. It seemed almost as though Jesus had walked across the surf to be with me, just as He walked the waters of Galilee to be with His disciples. In that moment, He was *present*—present there with *me;* and the ministering might of His presence lifted my burden and powerfully transformed my world—lifting the load of fear and pressure from my mind.

God had honored His promise through David to "inhabit the praises" of His people. Here, the Hebrew word for "inhabit" may also be translated "enthroned," opening the passage to show us its meaning: *God creates a dwelling place among those who praise Him.* It doesn't specify whether the worshiper need be hurting or joyful at the moment, but it's moving to note the text as one where the praiser is at a point of despair.

Here is a magnificent truth! Just as God is sovereign whether we worship Him or not, He will indwell us mightily and majestically whether we are feeling happy or sad—*when we praise Him*. Praise constructs a Throne room in our hearts where the Sovereign God declares He is pleased to dwell.

Despite any burden or pressure you may have brought to this moment, let me encourage you to open your heart and worship Him who invites you: "Come to Me, all you who labor and are heavy laden, and I will give you rest" (Matt. 11:28). Answer with worship and the miracle will occur, for it is in worship that you and I will discover anew that "the tabernacle of God is with men" (Rev. 21:3).

Praise in Prayer

God enthroned above, I praise You for dwelling also in my own heart. You know what makes me weep even before I do. Lift my vision above my burdens, and enable me to live in the power of praise. Through Christ our Lord, Amen.

Selected Readings

| Psalm 22:1-21 | John 14:1-6 |
| Psalm 103:1-18 | Hebrews 12:1-6 |

Praise in Practice

1. Imagine bringing a problem, wrapped in a "burden bundle," to the throne of Jesus. Picture Him reaching out and offering to take it. Does the picture include your being all too glad to turn it over to Him, or do you

imagine yourself hesitating? Are you aware of any reluctance? Do you fear what might be required of you if you let Him bear the burden? Remember that *trust* is a part of praise.

2. Recall the burden Christ bore to the cross—the sins of the world. Compare any burdens you may have just now with that. This isn't to show that your own burden is trivial, but to help put your life in perspective...to view it from the standpoint of the Cross.

3. Set aside a few moments—just five or ten minutes each day—in which you can think quietly about only the "praise points" or blessings in your life. You may want to include these reflections on the Psalms in these quiet times.

5

Come Before His Presence with Thinking, *Too*

"I will extol You, my God, O King; and I will bless Your name forever and ever....Great is the Lord, and greatly to be praised; and His greatness is unsearchable."—Psalm 145:1,3

The psalmist had a very pointed reason to dwell on God's unfathomable greatness, for all about him the gods of a pagan world were being recommended as a superior alternative to the true God. But the writer extols God's greatness in contrast to these very idols. He resonates to the same Spirit prompting the writer of Psalm 135: "For I know that the Lord is great, and our Lord is above all gods" (vs. 5). The Bible hymn writers are careful to point us on a path that takes to mind the deficiencies of lying "gods," the world's deceptive systems—and how the true God by contrast is our God, towering high above all competitors.

It's a wise discipline. I suspect that giving more thought to just *how* God is greater than the world's idol systems, we would be more effective in confronting and overcoming the idolatries of our private world. But such confrontation *does* take thought—and our worship is a worthy time for turning our hearts and minds whole-heartedly to the task. Unfortunately, however, too many people too easily come to think that it's enough just to "praise the Lord" in a near-mindless, so-called relaxed, laid-back way, which parks their capacity for reasoned thought at the door of the sanctuary, or upon entering *any* worship time.

But the Bible insists that worship includes our entire being. In Romans 12:1, the apostle Paul says that serving God involves our "reasonable" faculties, and he uses the very Greek term from which we derive our word "logic" (Rom. 12:1). He challenges us to *renew our minds* (vs. 2); to worship not only in spirit but in *truth* (John 4:24). We will later note God's call to "Come before His presence with singing," but here we should note that we are also to come before Him with *thinking*. Hear Paul again: "I will sing with the spirit, and I will also sing with the understanding"—that is, with thought-filled song! (1 Cor. 14:15).

Thinking carefully about the attributes of God as we praise Him is a way of offering Him our minds. When we hear the psalmist say that God is "above all gods," let's try to wrap our minds around His *omnipotence*—the fact that He is all powerful. What a staggering intellectual concept! Employ your mind also to contemplate God's *omnipresence*—that He is everywhere present. He's inescapably, marvelously near, all at once; not a mere human dwelling on a mountaintop or a pagan god propped in a shrine. Nor is He a local deity, like the "gods" of the world order superstitiously worshiped as with Laban (Gen. 31:19ff). And think further on *our* God—the *one* God who alone is *omniscient*—knowing all there is to know, now or forever. What an absolutely mind-boggling thought, as are all these attributes which thinking on His greatness bring to mind.

In short, the call to worship doesn't mean to roll back your eyes and let your mind turn to mush. Yet, in using our minds we should never make the mistake we are to ascend some intellectual throne. Thought-filled worship should drive us to our knees! The intellect should bow us in worship instead of lifting us in pride. When we think straight, we will humble ourselves before the One who so greatly transcends our own capacity for intellect, and adore the God who is not only above all gods but above all that we will ever grasp or think.

Praise in Prayer

O God, You are Lord of my mind as well as my heart. You know my deepest questions, and even though the answers are not clear to me, I praise You even through my questions. Help me to submit my mind to You in love and service. Through Jesus, Amen.

Selected Readings

Proverbs 4:1-9   Romans 12:1-3
Romans 11:33-36   1 Corinthians 1:18-25

Praise in Practice

1. Ask yourself, or discuss in a group, whether the human intellect is more often used to draw people *away* from God or *closer* to Him. Name specific ways.

2. Do hard questions—such as why people seem to suffer unjustly, or why our prayers aren't always answered—stand in the way of your offering total commitment to God in worship or in life? Write a question like this on a 3×5 card, beginning it with the words, "I wonder why...?" Then write below the question Psalm 145:3—"Great is the Lord, and greatly to be praised; and His greatness is unsearchable." Carry this note with you for a day or two, taking it out and reading it frequently to affirm that God is not only above idols, but above all questions, too. Practice "praising God anyway"—ascribing glory to Him even in the midst of your unanswered questions.

6

On Not Being Lonely Even When Alone

"A father of the fatherless, a defender of widows, is God in His holy habitation. God sets the solitary in families; He brings out those who are bound into prosperity."—Psalm 68:5,6

Those who live alone—single adults, those who have lost a beloved family member, widows and widowers, people who have simply been abandoned—can sometimes feel so isolated and estranged and lonely that it's easy to feel abandoned by God as well. Here the psalmist calls us to worship the One who personally knows and loves us. And we're shown how God wants to help us see that He delights to "set the solitary in families" through healthy Christian fellowship.

I was once struggling through the genealogy in the first chapter of Matthew, and found myself thinking, *What an uninteresting way to begin the New Testa-*

ment—with lists and lists of names. But as I paused to inquire of the Lord, praying for insight, it occurred to me that God has put such lists of names in the Bible for at least three reasons: (1) He cares about and remembers individual people, and calls them by name; (2) He makes promises to people, and keeps them; and (3) He accomplishes His purpose in imperfect people and through fallible people.

God asserts His "knowing" us individually, being able to see our "frame" in the womb even before birth, when we were "yet unformed" (Ps. 139:15,16). It is because God *does* keep us specifically on His mind—personally—that He knows the exact number of hairs on our head (Matt. 10:30). If God did not literally see and know you and me, love us each individually even when we feel isolated from Him as well as from people, Paul wouldn't have affirmed Jesus' death being "for *me*, not only died for the whole world*" (Gal. 2:20). But our text adds to this, showing how "God goes even further than individual care. He works at "grouping" us so loneliness can be removed from our lives.

God has set us in "the family"—the Church—partly because we need each other. I need you to help complete what I'm to become, and you need me and the several others in the fellowship who can touch your life. You see, all of us—single or "joined"—need not only to be reborn but to be *rebuilt.* Not everyone contributes in the same way and sometimes, some people may seem more a liability than an asset to your building program. But the Word of God reminds us, that "none of us lives to himself, and no one dies to himself" (Rom. 14:7).

34

This one verse summarizes a biblical principle which is far more than a mere social commentary regarding mutual goodwill. It is a conclusive statement from the Holy Spirit teaching us that our lives are irrevocably integrated in the affairs of others. If you try to avoid learning what God wants to do through those relationships, you withdraw at your own expense. You'll be poorer for having done so.

After saying this we should also acknowledge that not everyone who is alone is lonely. As is often said, "One is a *whole* number." Some people have found that "flying solo" can bring the riches of solitude instead of the poverty of loneliness. Sometimes such people who have come to terms with themselves as whole persons are the best equipped for the interactions of fellowship with others—they know better than some where the boundaries of the personality are.

Still, all of us, however capably we handle our lives, need people. That's why God has set the solitary in His spiritual family—to help each of us help nurture and rebuild each other. Our growth and healing depend on it!

Praise in Prayer

Dear Father, the world is so large, and even crowds can be so lonely, I need Your companionship, and the love of brothers and sisters. Help me not to resist the very way You have planned for me to grow. In the name of Jesus I pray, Amen.

Selected Readings

Exodus 22:21-24   1 Corinthians 12:12-22
Romans 15:1-7   Ephesians 4:11-15

Praise in Practice

1. Do you ever have feelings of loneliness—whether you're single or living in a local family? Do you have interest areas or questions or needs in which you feel no one shares? Make a point to explore the possibility that others in your circle of acquaintances have similar needs. It may be that they are just reluctant to say so.

2. If you live in a family, plan to invite one or more singles to a meal or an outing. If you live alone, plan a similar time with someone else in your spiritual family.

3. Look up the word "xenophobia" in a dictionary. What do you think causes it? What might cure it?

7

Come to the Feast!

*"You prepare a table before me in the presence
of my enemies; You anoint my head with oil;
my cup runs over."*—Psalm 23:5

In ancient Israel, mealtime took on special significance
when guests were present. You were careful about who
you faced across the table, for dining together was a
sign of acceptance and fellowship. Sometimes the meal
would even be a celebration of a covenant. After all,
Israel could trace its very existence to the Passover meal
in Egypt. And their covenant with God had been sealed
by Moses and the other leaders by eating and drinking
(Exod. 24:11).

The table spread for the psalmist here in this famous
psalm was remarkable for still another reason: It was
spread in the presence of King David's enemies. Imagine—those who had sought David's life had to sit by
and watch him actually share a banquet with the God
who protected him!

As believers in Jesus, we recreate this scene whenever we gather for worship around the Lord's Table. In the Communion, the setting of praise is public. It's a table Christ Himself has spread so openly that even enemies of the faith—visible *or* invisible—can witness the table fellowship we enjoy with Christ. While private times of worship and praise are important, nothing can take the place of this periodic banquet with Christ and other Christians.

At the table, as with Israel amid its taskmakers in Egypt, for the Passover lamb we have been given the Lamb of God Himself. "This is my body," Jesus said, as He broke the unleavened bread at the Last Supper. For us, the term "body" recalls both the physical body of Christ that was broken on the cross, and the Church, "which is His Body" (Eph. 1:22,23). Thus, at His Table, we not only think of Christ's sacrifice at Communion, but we are also mindful of our union with each other. The church at Corinth forgot this "people" aspect of "Body," ignoring the poor among them, and the apostle Paul said that this carelessness prevented them from sharing the Supper acceptably (see 1 Cor. 11:23,24). Let us be wisely warned.

And let us also remember Jesus' words, "This is my blood." In the wine of Communion we participate with each other and with our Lord in the very essence of that which saves us—the blood of Jesus Christ, which cleanses us from all sin!

What outbursts of praise this should call forth from Christians! Let's never allow the Lord's Supper to degenerate into a morbid memory, a dull routine or a rote ritual. Here is the meal that we share with Him who delivered us and our kinfolk, Israel, from bondage. We celebrate the sacrifice of our Lord on the cross on behalf of the sins of the world. And we affirm that Jesus will come again, for we anticipate the ultimate "last" Last Supper—the Messianic banquet that we will enjoy not in holy isolation, but in the heavenly joyous presence of our Savior and the saved of all ages!

Praise in Prayer

What a joy, O God, to be invited to the feast of good things we celebrate in the Lord's Supper! I praise You for the sacrifice that makes this possible...for filling me to the brim and running over...and for brothers and sisters who share this banquet with me. In the name of Christ our Passover, Amen.

Selected Readings

Exodus 12:1-14   Matthew 26:17-30
Isaiah 25:1-9   1 Corinthians 11:17-34

Praise in Practice

1. Think about or discuss in a group how the "horizontal" or "Body Life" dimension of the Lord's Supper could be emphasized where you worship.

2. List on a 3×5 card several specific blessings you enjoy as a direct result of Christ's having offered Himself

on the cross. Think not only of the forgiveness of sins, but of blessings such as fellowship with specific people in the Body, and other riches that enable you to say "My cup runneth over." Carry the card with you throughout a day at work, taking it out frequently to remind yourself of the "feast" of good things you enjoy in Christ.

8

All You Need Is a Broken Heart

"For You do not desire sacrifice, or else I would give it; You do not delight in burnt offering. The sacrifices of God are a broken spirit, a broken and a contrite heart."—Psalm 51:16,17

I love laughter and song and just plain joyfulness as much as anyone. Yet there is a "forced" happiness among some church folk that makes me uncomfortable. You know the line—"You just lost your job? Well, praise God for that, brother!" Or, "My mother is dying of cancer, but I'm still just praising the Lord."

Not only can this kind of response be a study in "religiously" generated dishonesty, but it can cause some people overhearing such talk to think that if they can't bring themselves to make such glib affirmations, then they're in no position—or disposition—to worship or exercise the power of faith. The truth is, true worship may *result* in happiness or bright emotions, but it is subject to the entire range of human feeling, including the "broken heart," such as David describes his bringing to God in this text.

In one sense brokenness is the very essence of worship. It was physically required when animals were slain in Old Testament worship, for the "perfect" sacrifices were "broken" when slain. They were not only a substitute atonement for the sin of the worshiper, but were a sacrifice of self. The gift of "life" indicated that the worshiper was giving up his own interests; sacrificing his ownership of an animal in honor of the superior "worthship" of God. That's why the animal could not be crippled or blemished, for such an offering, being worthless, would reflect on the worthiness of God, and would demonstrate a less than sincere or full understanding on the part of the worshiper (see Lev. 1:2,3).

Unfortunately, the fact that these sacrifices were costly led some to think that the more expensive the gift the more God would be pleased, and that thus, the greater the worshiper would be blessed. But God was interested in the worshiper's heartfelt *obedience*—in the attitude of heart represented by the *offering*—not solely in who could afford to bring the most oxen or sheep to the altar. This, of course, is what led David to affirm the beautiful truth of Psalm 51:17.

The story surrounding the text emphasizes this truth dramatically. Remember the depth of David's sin, his adultery with Bathsheba, and his gross attempt to cover it up with her husband Uriah's murder. As a wealthy king, David could have afforded to offer thousands of oxen or sheep or goats, but there weren't enough animals in the world to compensate for his sin. No altar could have been built large enough to receive enough animal sacrifices. It was David's *heart* that had been closed to the will of God and sinned so willfully. But now, opening it in a will to heartfelt repentance, the king humbly asks for a new capacity to praise: "O Lord, open my lips, and my mouth shall show forth Your praise" (vs. 15).

This is when David received this remarkable revelation of the sacrifice God really wants: All you need is a broken heart! Ultimately, it's not the sight of an animal sacrifice that moves God to grant forgiveness and to receive David back into His embrace. It is David's broken heart—the spirit that had grown tender enough to be pained by sin.

There's no need to be embarrassed if you can't bring God a jolly heart every time you feel the need to praise Him. There's no shame in not being able to afford an expensive gift as though you could "buy God off" and purchase forgiveness. Just bring Him your heart, broken though it may be. That's what He has wanted all along.

Praise in Prayer

I give You my heart as Lord of my life, O God. Even when I am sorrowful...even when I am less than I want to be...I praise You as a God who accepts the open and honest heart over any material sacrifice I could bring. In the name of Christ my Savior, Amen.

Selected Readings

Psalm 51:10-19   Luke 18:9-14
Amos 5:21-27   Hebrews 10:18-23

Praise in Practice

1. In your own experience, are people more likely to praise God when they are "up," or when they are painfully aware of their shortcomings?

2. The psalmist said in Psalm 77:3, "I remembered God, and was troubled." Some people find it surprising to learn that thinking about God doesn't always produce a happy heart. Read this verse in context—Psalm 77:1-9—and think about or discuss the reasons for the psalmist's sadness. Was his mood appropriate?

3. Notice also that the psalmist doesn't *stay* in such depression. Read verses 10-15, and describe the specific steps the psalmist took to move from sorrow to praise.

9

How Much Does God Weigh?

"The heavens declare the glory of God; and the firmament shows His handiwork."—Psalm 19:1
"Let the whole earth be filled with His glory."
—Psalm 72:19

In a very literal sense, the Psalms are glorious! They are not only glorious in the sense of joyous wonder, but they are also filled with examples of God's *glory*—expressions that glorify Him and admonitions to worshipers to ascribe to God the glory that is due Him. "Glory" is such an important idea in the Psalms, let's focus on it for a pair of devotions.

What does it mean to say that God is glorious?

Our answer in part is found in the basic meaning of the Old Testament word most often translated "glory." It is *chabod*, a word that basically refers, surprisingly enough, to "weight" or "substance." For example, the same root word is used to describe poor Eli, an over-weight priest whose death is recorded in 1 Samuel 4:12-18. Eli was perched up on a high seat—perhaps in one of the watchtowers erected by guards to protect a vine-yard, or atop a wall or gatepost; he was there awaiting news of the battle in which Israel was engaged. Because Israel's people had been unfaithful, they not only lost the battle, but the ark of God was captured, too. When Eli heard this devastating news he apparently suffered a stroke. At least he was so stunned that he fell from his seat and broke his neck, for he "was old and *[chabod]* heavy" (vs. 18).

But what can weight or heaviness have to do with *God's* glory? Surely He isn't "overweight"! Then again, maybe He *is*—possibly in the colloquial sense as when a concept is *profound*, and someone might say, "That's *heavy!*"

There's the connection. Because there is no *concept* or *thought* or *being* quite as "heavy" or profoundly glo-rious as God. He is the most "substantial" fact in all reality. Sometimes people make the mistake of thinking that only what they can touch or see, taste or feel—what we call the realm of substance—is the "real" world. But this is the foundational point of human con-fusion—one might say, the beginning point of "sub-stance" abuse!

To help us avoid such confusion about reality, Psalm 19:1 says that the very existence of the heavens and the sky testifies to the *true* "substance"—the "glory" or the *substantial nature* of God. "The real world" not only was *made* by God, but it testifies to Him. We are never so much "in the real world" as when ascribing to God the glory or "weight of substantial worthiness" due Him!

Another meaning of *chabod* (glory) is "honor." For example, have you ever been in a courtroom when the judge entered, and everyone stood? Or in a room where a head of state drew everyone to their feet just by making an entrance? In some countries people even kneel or bow before royal personages. These are gestures showing the "weight" we give to the presence of those whom we honor. So the psalmist sings, "Make a joyful shout to God, all the earth! Sing out the honor *[chabod]* of His name; make His praise glorious *[chabod]*" (Ps. 66:1,2).

Does God carry more "weight" with you than any*thing* else, or any*one* else, in the world?

Praise in Prayer

God of grace and God of glory, help me grant You the weight and the space in my life that is due You. I do glorify You as King of all kings and Lord of all lords, through Jesus Christ my Savior, Amen.

Selected Readings

Exodus 24:9-18   Luke 2:8-20
Psalm 19   Revelation 21:9-27

Praise in Practice

1. Thumb through a hymnbook and note the ones

that speak specifically of God's glory, or of glorifying Him. As you read titles and phrases in these hymns, think of "glory" as "substance" or "weight" or "real value," and note whether it heightens the hymn's intent to glorify God.

2. Sing a couple of these songs, such as "To God Be the Glory," "Be Glorified" or "Glorious Things of Thee Are Spoken."

3. How do you define "the real world"? If you had to label your view, would you call it materialism? Idealism? Another term? Are any such labels really adequate for the biblical view?

10

God's Glory and Man's Conduct

"Whoever offers praise glorifies Me; and to him who orders his conduct aright I will show the salvation of God."—Psalm 50:23

What connection is there between glorifying God and ordering our conduct or behavior aright? As we just learned, "glory" is related to the idea of *substance* or *weight*. When we glorify God do we increase His honor or "weight"? Is He so insecure that He pouts and sulks until we tell Him how great He is?

Obviously not. God is who He is, whether we confess it, sing it, declare it or not! Only He can say, "The world is Mine, and all its fullness," and only He can say, "If I were hungry, I would not tell you" (Ps. 50:12). Paul emphasized this same truth, telling pagan worshipers that the true God "is not served by human hands, as if he needed anything" (Acts 17:25, *NIV*). No, it is not God who is affected or changed when we glorify Him; *we* are.

When we honor and glorify God, praising Him for the "weight" He carries with us, something wonderful begins to happen to us. We are *changed* under this weight. Not surprisingly, dwelling under the "glorious" or "weighty" God will put pressure on us, but not the kind of "pressure" we humans produce—wearying and stress-filled. Rather, God's "weight" is a kind of healthy, healing or *shaping* influence, the same as that which a potter impresses on clay. God's weight of glory shapes us into vessels far more honorable and profitable than if we did not subject ourselves to His loving influence. This is why our text relates *right conduct* to *glory*.

A beautiful illustration of this principle at work is given in 2 Corinthians 4:16,17. The apostle Paul notes that although growing older seems, outwardly, to be a gradual "perishing," believers find their inner spirits "renewed day by day." How does this happen? By the influence of this "weight of glory."

You may know older Christians who are living examples of this process. Even though their bodies are declining, you've seen in them a beautiful spirit that seems to get more Christlike the older they get. What is happening here? They have simply led lives that so glorified God that their own spirits have been gradually molded "into the same image." The weight of glory has shaped them; more and more they resemble their Father. This is a lifelong process, and irrespective of age, it's happening in you and me *now!*

A negative example of the same principle appears in

Romans 1. Here Paul describes how low people can sink morally. Why did it happen? "Because, although they knew God, they did not *glorify* Him as God" (vs. 21, and see the rest of Romans 1, emphasis mine). Once again we see how worship affects conduct. As we said in the beginning, worship changes the worshiper into the image of the One worshiped.

How privileged we are! Honored to have the impress of His glory upon us as we are being made into people of right conduct as we walk a path of ascribing glory and honor to God!

Praise in Prayer

Dear Lord, I long to glorify You in ways that not only bring honor to Your name, but also transform my conduct, and enable me to grow into the image of Your Son. Please help me to be responsive to the working of Your Holy Spirit in molding me and shaping me into the kind of worshiper who best glorifies You. I pray through Jesus, Amen.

Selected Readings

1 Chronicles 29:26-30	Psalm 59
Psalm 58	1 Corinthians 3:17,18

Praise in Practice

1. Are you aware of any positive changes in your life

since you began to be a genuine believer, glorifying God? On the other hand, what improvement in your conduct do you yet hope to make as you live under "the weight of glory"?

2. The idea of being fashioned "into the same image" of Christ is often called "sanctification." Using a concordance and a Bible dictionary, discuss the various aspects of this term.

3. Discuss the implications of Matthew 11:28-30, in the light of God's glory being, in one sense, "weight."

11

How to Know God's Will for Your Life

"The secret of the Lord is with those who fear Him, and He will show them His covenant."
—Psalm 25:14

Religion is often associated with secret knowledge. Bible historians describe a style of thinking called "gnostic," a religious philosophy that was very prevalent in New Testament times. The word "gnostic" is from the Greek *gnosis* for knowledge. The ancient movement's appeal was that if you decided to go with them you would "learn secret words," "see secret things," "be initiated into a fellowship of secret rites." It appealed to human pride, to those who sought an elite order of relationship with the supernatural.

But the psalmist holds to the contrary, that God's secrets are not revealed to an elite, but to those who fear Him—those who honor, respect and obey Him.

One new version translates the verse in a more personal way, saying that "The Lord confides in those who fear him" (NIV). Imagine being the confidant of the Creator and Sustainer of the universe, in whom lie all of life's secrets! Think of being able to know the will of Him who "does great things which we cannot comprehend" (Job 37:5); knowing the One who knows "by what way is light diffused," and "from whose womb comes the ice?" (38:24,29).

In short, the point is that the primary part of God's master plan for the ages is an open book to those who enter into covenant with Him, for that plan is *Jesus!* You don't have to be initiated into a secret society to relate to the God of the Bible. There are no secret formulas or magical words to learn. In fact, much of the New Testament was written to combat this very kind of thinking.

Paul warns Timothy, his son in the faith, to avoid "the profane and vain babblings and contradictions of what is falsely called knowledge" (the word here is *gnosis*). He continues by noting that those who profess it, "have strayed concerning the faith" (1 Tim. 6:20,21). Throughout the whole of the New Covenant Scriptures, inspired writers insist that God has revealed His whole plan for the ages through Jesus Christ: "This thing was not done in a corner" (Acts 26:26). Christian life and the life of worship, then, is not mystical or magical. It's lived and expressed in the light, not in secret meeting places or dark, secluded caves.

God reveals His covenant to anyone who is willing to believe in His Son, trusts Him enough to accept Him, and then has the humility to walk and grow in a reverent childlike spirit; always confessing that without Him they *don't* know the way...at all!

If you feel a hunger or desire for more specific knowledge of God's Person or His will for your life, check the depth and integrity of your worship and service—the specifics of fearing the Lord. In Romans 12:1,2, Paul indicates that this kind of wholehearted worship means to "present your bodies a living sacrifice, holy, acceptable to God." And he teaches that it's in this kind of whole-life commitment, not in learning supernatural secrets withheld from others, "that you may prove what is that good and acceptable and perfect will of God."

Praise in Prayer

I praise You, O God, for revealing Your plan for the ages through Jesus Christ, and for entrusting me with that revelation. Help me to discern Your voice above the clamor of life, and to honor and reverence You in order to be Your close companion and confidant. Through Christ, Amen.

Selected Readings

Job 38:1-11   1 Corinthians 2:1-10
Isaiah 35   1 Corinthians 8:1-3

Praise in Practice

1. What differences are there between wanting to

know about God, and actually *fearing* Him (in the Bible sense of having reverence for Him)?

2. Are there particular areas of your life for which you long to know more about God's will? If you're comfortable doing so, share them with others and invite the input of other believers.

3. What guidelines can you suggest for discerning God's specific will? How can we distinguish His voice from the voice of others, or that of our own self-interest?

4. In your daily routine, be sure to include a time for being quiet before the Lord and listening for Him to speak His will. Perhaps this is a good time and place now for doing this, individually or as a group.

12
Where Does God Live?

*"You are holy, who inhabit the praises of
Israel. Our fathers trusted in You; they trusted,
and You delivered them."*—Psalm 22:3,4

What an intriguing fact-promise the psalmist expresses
here! It's as though he is answering the question, Where
does God dwell? The answer is: *God lives in the praises
of His people.* Let me share a very personal experience
connected with The Church On The Way, where I minister, that illustrates this strange but powerful statement.

I believe sincerely that God has graciously allowed
me to see a visible manifestation of His presence—
twice. The first time was years ago, at the end of a
counseling session. I had had a very fruitful conversation with a young student in my office. Before leaving,
we sat with bowed heads, just enjoying a quiet moment
and asking God's blessing on what had been said. Suddenly I opened my eyes and noticed that the room was
aglow with a silvery mist—a soft, shimmering haze that

reminded me of the cloud over the Tabernacle that signified God's presence during the ministry of Moses.

There was no smog or natural mist in the air—even though it was Los Angeles! I wondered if it was an illusion. But as I looked and saw the young person also marveling at the silvery remarkable scene, I knew what we were seeing was real. Our eyes met, and we simply nodded in silent agreement that God had blessed us with a very special moment, an indication of His presence. I had never experienced anything like it before; but there was one occasion like it several months later.

When my wife and I began pastoring the small handful of people who became The Church On The Way, we were trying to "find our way"; to fit in with whatever God had in mind for us. Most strongly impressed on us was the need to build on a solid foundation of worship. We wanted more than anything else to conduct our gatherings in a way that invited God's presence. We determined not to be limited by anything we had inherited from our church tradition that didn't contribute to worshiping in the way God wanted us to. "Worship as priority" was to be our emphasis. God was faithful to bless our efforts, and we grew. Which brings me to the next time I saw the strange glow.

It was nearly two years into this pastorate that one Saturday I had left my office to go home, having finished preparing for the Sunday morning services. As I looked across the sanctuary, suddenly that same silvery haze filled the room, the soft mist similar to what I had seen before. God's Word of John 17, Jesus' promise to "give His glory to His Church," confirmed my otherwise reticent response. I knew this was the awesome presence of God, showing us that, just as the psalmist said, God is fully ready to dwell among people who determine to be a people of genuine worship.

I know you will understand that I could never share this story with you in arrogance, or in the belief that the congregation I serve has "arrived." Rather, I am convinced that we will always have much to learn, continually, as we learn and live in true worship. I am also convinced that the *order* of things which happened to us can happen to you: that in *His* way at *your* place He will manifest Himself. To invite that, let your heart be filled with God, and fill your life with His praise.

He's prepared to "inhabit" *your* praises in very real ways, too.

Praise in Prayer

You are present everywhere, at all times, O God. Yet we long to experience your life, love and power in all those ways—special ways that will please you. Bless our attempts to worship You acceptably, and open the eyes of our hearts so we may see Your ways and welcome Your inhabiting of our praises, Amen.

Selected Readings

Psalm 68:32-35   Acts 17:22-31
Psalm 139:7-12   Revelation 21:1-3

Praise in Practice

1. Describe any experience you may have had when God's presence seemed so real it could be felt—or even seen.

2. Can physical appointments in a sanctuary, or attempts to create "atmosphere," create God's presence? If not, what is necessary for this experience?

13

Let All That Is in Me Cry, "Holy!"

"Vindicate me, O Lord, for I have walked in my integrity. I have also trusted in the Lord; I shall not slip. Examine me, O Lord, and prove me; try my mind and my heart."
—Psalm 26:1,2

The concept of integrity in this psalm is interesting in connection with the praise and worship of God. Certainly David isn't claiming to be sinless, for he had already confessed his sin; but he rises to declare His integrity. This English word, from the same root as our word *integer,* meaning a whole number, is expressive of David's asserting that God had made him a whole person in his life-style and relationships. When confronted with sin, he confessed, and repented. He did not want to keep a part of himself from God. All that was in him cried "Holy!"—that is, "God, let Your holy completeness fill in and fill out the broken and hollow places carved or eroded by my sin and failure!"

The wisdom of New Testament worship is that it isn't just a head trip, a mystical consciousness or an emotional binge. It is our *whole* person coming before the *Holy* God to be made fully holy and whole—aglow with the life of the Spirit. Paul said it plainly enough in 1 Thessalonians 5:23:

> Now may the God of peace Himself sanctify you [wholly, *KJV*] completely;...your whole spirit, soul, and body...at the coming of our Lord Jesus Christ.

Let us then worship with a *regenerated spirit,* connecting the eternal part of our beings with the Eternal Spirit of God. Let us worship with a *renewed mind,* seeking to know as fully as we can the God whom we worship. Let us praise God with *revived emotions,* not allowing pseudo-sophistication to make us too embarrassed for passionate praise. And let us not be afraid to worship God with a *rededicated body,* placing it, as it were, on the altar of sacrifice as well as incorporating appropriate postures in our worship.

Now, we've all probably been in some services where worshiping God with the physical body seemed out of place. I have no desire to put down anyone's Christian heritage—there are very understandable historical reasons for the different Christian traditions of worship. But I can't help but point out that if we ever reduce worship to a purely mental action, we're going against the grain not only of Scripture but of what we know about human nature as well.

For years now, authorities in both physical and mental health fields have remarked on the need to integrate the whole nature of our persons in our practical life. This is but the start of what the Bible means when the word "holy" is used. It's related to "whole"—to our *whole*-hearted response to God's *holy* claim on us. It is an integrating of the reality of the realm of the spirit, the realm of the physical and the realm of the mind and the realm of the body. Holy wholeness! Whole holiness!

Let us then also acknowledge the wholesomeness and holiness of worshiping with body, soul and spirit. There's a very good reason for it: God wants *all* of you in His service—not just your head, not just your heart, but your hands to do His bidding, your feet to run His race, your entire body as a spiritual sacrifice.

Praise in Prayer

Dear Heavenly Father, I praise You for the whole creation, for the material as well as the spiritual world. Help me to present my whole being— thoughts, words, emotions and actions as a living sacrifice in my worship and living. Through Jesus' love I pray, Amen.

Selected Readings

John 5:1-14 (*KJV*)   1 Thessalonians 5:23,24
John 13:1-11   James 1:21-27

Praise in Practice

1. Do you find it embarrassing to be demonstrative in worship—as in raising your hands in prayer? Why or why not? How about bowing the head? Kneeling? Think about and discuss your feelings about these ways of "worshiping with the body."

2. What parallel between worship "with the whole person" and Christian living does this chapter suggest?

3. For many people, Christianity as a "merely mental" matter or idea extends not only to worship but to their concept of heaven. But what do you think the apostle Paul meant by the concept of our having a "spiritual body" in the world to come? (See 1 Cor. 15:35-55.)

14

With My Hands Lifted Up

"Because Your lovingkindness is better than life, my lips shall praise You. Thus I will bless You while I live; I will lift up my hands in Your name"—Psalm 63:3,4

Continuing our theme of worshiping God in body, soul, mind and spirit, we note here that the psalmist threw himself "lips and hands" into praising God! He illustrates the time-honored practice of extending the hands upward in worship. In the name of being modern, have we ever felt too sophisticated to do as the psalmist did? Can we not follow the apostle Paul's admonition, "Pray everywhere, lifting up holy hands" (1 Tim. 2:8)?

The beautifully expressive hands of the Hawaiian dancer, or the signer to mutes or the deaf, are eloquent illustrations of the fact that we do not communicate merely with the tongue. Millions have marveled at the expressiveness in Albrecht Dürer's engraving "Praying Hands," their appreciation for it sharpened when they hear that they were the hands of Dürer's brother, who earned a living at rude, rough work in order for Albrecht to study art.

Hands "speak volumes" in Christian worship, too. The upward reach of worshiping hands is a confession that God is "above" us—not in the spatial sense (the report of the first Russian cosmonaut that he hadn't seen God in space, implying that He therefore doesn't exist is of course based on such a pathetic misunderstanding). But rather, we acknowledge God's "above-ness" as a confession of His divine superiority. The outstretched hands turned palm outward in praise may signal our *extending* to God our praise and our love; while hands turned palm upward in worship seem to express our plea for more and more of the filling of His Holy Spirit.

Notice that the psalmist speaks of God's lovingkindness being "better than life" in the same breath as his statement about worshiping with uplifted hands. It's not that he does not appreciate his temporal life, but in worship he reaches for more of God's dimensions of life. Remember that "the gift of eternal life" promised the believer is not just life *unending*, but it is also life *unlimited*. It is life like that of the eternal God's, eternal in *quantity* but also eternal in *quality* since He presently infuses us with the traits of His lovingkindness. That's worth reaching for!

There is something exhilarating and liberating about standing with arms upstretched in worship. Gone are the limitations of merely "horizontal" life, with its misunderstandings and miscommunication in human speech, for in worshipful prayer the Spirit expresses our unspeakable longings (Rom. 8:26). Gone are the inhibitions and intimidation we experience in so much human interaction, for we are reaching for intimacy with God as a baby lifts its arms to a loving parent. Reaching toward the skies we may also confess our willingness to grow heavenward, refusing to be confined to earth-bound sordidness. The openness of upstretched arms can—indeed, should!—speak of all this.

Praise in Prayer

I reach up to You, O Father, acknowledging Your greatness, asking for more of You in my life, and putting myself in a position of growth and ever-expanding consciousness of and availability to You and Your will in my life, Amen.

Selected Readings

Psalm 63:3,4   Psalm 141:1-4
Psalm 134   Lamentations 3:37-41

Praise in Practice

1. If you're not a regular "hand-raiser," and feel a little awkward about it, try going outdoors on a comfortable night and lifting your hands upward to the heavens. No one sees you (as though that really mattered!). You're away from distractions and inhibitions. What

does the experience make you want to say to God?

2. Let's suppose it does matter "what people think." What do you think a non-Christian, not prejudiced one way or the other, would think is signified by upraised hands in a Christian worship service?

3. A book on worship by Robert Webber has the intriguing title, *Worship Is a Verb*. What does this title imply, and how might it relate to the topic of this chapter?

15

Let Us Kneel Before the Lord Our God, Our Maker

"Oh come, let us worship and bow down; let us kneel before the Lord our Maker....Do not harden your hearts, as in the rebellion."
—Psalm 95:6,8

Let's think through the basic meaning of one of the New Testament's primary words for worship: *proskeuneo*, which means "to prostrate oneself," and refers to the custom of presenting oneself on the ground face down before the Holy Living God. It's a word obviously related to our "worship with the body" theme we're pursuing in this section.

Of course the essence of falling on one's face is more than laying the body down, but evidences a submission of our will—a sign that we totally forfeit self-will in favor of the will of the One before whom we prostrate ourselves. *Proskeuneo* worship therefore implies absolute submission to the Lord.

Kneeling is another biblical way to show this in worship. While I fully recommend times of being "on one's face" in private worship, it isn't very practical in a crowded sanctuary! Perhaps kneeling is more appropriate there. As with the psalm above, it is clear that kneeling also implies the submission of our will to God's. Kneeling is contrasted with rebelling against God, as the Israelites did during their wandering in the wilderness after the Exodus. The admonition is, "Do not harden your hearts or rebel"; instead, "let us kneel before the Lord our Maker."

I'll never forget the time I was visiting another church where I was to preach. I was seated on the platform at the front of the sanctuary when the local pastor began to lead the congregation in prayer. Suddenly I had the most distinct impression that God wanted me to kneel. Although it was more of an inner awareness than a voice, it was as strong as a shout. I had no question about what God wanted me to do.

But you know, I really did not want to kneel there, fearful of seeming ostentatious before a congregation I didn't know. Other excuses for ignoring the message ran through my mind: "The audience will think I'm trying to appear super-pious"..."It might distract them from focusing on God," etc. But when God tells you to do something, all the excuses in the world are pretty weak. I really don't like to just ignore it when He clearly tells me to do something! So with some chagrin I knelt there, in prayer, as I'd been told to do.

But after a moment I couldn't resist a peek. I had to see if my fears were justified, if the people were reacting. But I was doubly embarrassed for having hesitated, for not a single person was looking at me! All were focused on their own worship. It taught me a good lesson. As I look back on my lame reasoning and hesitation to let my worship express *physically,* I am reminded of what that dear Christian teacher and writer Ethel Barrett said: "We would worry a lot less about what people think of us if we realized how seldom they do."

Such incidents should also remind us that God's way is really best, no matter what others may think. At any rate, it's worth asking: Is the real reason I sometimes resist outward, visible expressions of worship because it's a threat to the preservation of my own pride? My will? Or am I foremost concerned with His glory and will?

Praise in Prayer

Dear Lord, I confess that I need more of the spirit of submission that is symbolized by prostrating myself before You. "Mold me and make me after Thy will, while I am waiting, yielded and still." Through Jesus Christ our Lord, Amen.

Selected Readings

Joshua 5:13-15   Isaiah 45:18-25
2 Chronicles 6:12-14   Philippians 2:5-11

Praise in Practice

1. Is kneeling a part of formal, "high church" liturgy, or only informal or "charismatic" worship? Why do you think it isn't done as much among many evangelical churches today as it was a generation or so ago?

2. What motivation is best for encouraging people to "fall on their face" before God, in the sense of totally submitting to His will?

16

I Will Sing of the Mercies of the Lord

"Sing out the honor of His name; make His praise glorious....All the earth shall worship You and sing praises to You; they shall sing praises to Your name."—Psalm 66:2,4

Both Judaism and Christianity are singing faiths. There are so many references to music and singing in the Psalms that they have been called Israel's "hymnbook." The word "psalm" actually means "song," originally referring to one sung to the accompaniment of a psaltery, an ancient stringed instrument. Psalm-singing was important from the very beginning of Christianity, especially to express the sheer exuberance and joy Christians experience: "Is anyone cheerful? Let him sing psalms" (Jas. 5:13).

Every period of renewal in Christian history has been accompanied with renewed interest in what believers sing. During periods of spiritual decline in the Middle Ages, monks were careful to preserve the psalms both in writing and singing. The work of Martin Luther in this area is well known. We still drink of the streams of the Reformation when we sing Luther's great hymn, "A Mighty Fortress Is Our God." During the Reformation in Scotland, the psalms, in rhythmic paraphrase, were a source of much of the sturdiness of Scottish faith.

We recall that King David, the author of so many of the psalms, was a singer and harpist himself. One of the Bible's earliest portraits of David depicts him playing and singing for King Saul, to calm the king's rages (1 Sam. 16:23). We can well imagine Saul's mad ravings subsiding under such reassuring lyrics as, "Whenever I am afraid, I will trust in You....I will not fear. What can flesh do to me?" (Ps. 56:3,4).

Part of the power of song is that it is a beautiful expression of devotion both for the solitary worshiper at private devotions, at work or in the car, and for the congregation gathered for public worship. People can make no more expressive sounds than in song. Singing releases the pent-up joy and thanksgiving we feel because of God's grace and goodness; so the psalmist sings, "To You, O my Strength, I will sing praises" (Ps. 59:17). In singing we can also teach and admonish each other: "Do not be drunk with wine, in which is dissipation; but be filled with the Spirit, speaking to one another in psalms and hymns and spiritual songs, singing and making melody in your heart to the Lord" (Eph. 5:18,19).

74

You say you don't have a good voice? You don't know music? Both can be developed but never without "singing anyway"! Remember, *God* likes your voice; and even if you never learn to carry a tune, use it. You carry around with you the most important instrument for singing: *your heart.* Make melody in and with it!

Praise in Prayer

Our hearts sometimes feel they will burst, O Lord, with joy and thanksgiving for Your gifts and grace. Thank You for allowing us to express this in song, and for those who can inspire us with music. Accept our own singing, however imperfect, for the melody in our hearts, Amen.

Selected Readings

Exodus 15:1-21   Romans 15:7-13
Judges 5   Revelation 15:1-4

Praise in Practice

1. If you know these songs, or have access to them in a hymnbook, sing, "I Will Sing unto the Lord" and "Sing Hallelujah to His Name."

2. Do you think that the music at the church where you worship is a good ministry to the Lord and upbuilding for the worshipers? If not, what positive and constructive changes can you suggest?

3. What are some of your favorite hymns? Why do

you appreciate them—because they are "old favorites," because of their message, because of the mood or tone they set?

4. Without letting this session degenerate into an argument, what do you think about contemporary Christian music, especially Christian rock music?

17
Singing Against the Night

"I am so troubled that I cannot speak. I have considered the days of old, the years of ancient times. I call to remembrance my song in the night."—Psalm 77:4-6

Continuing our thinking about singing and the worship of God, let's shift the focus from the emphasis in the last chapter about song as a joyful outlet for praise and thanksgiving to less joyful times. We've mentioned before that praise is not just for our "happy times" but the sad, as well. Drawing from the wisdom of David and the Psalms, we are invited to enter a curious fortress of strength. In the passage cited above, the worshiper sings even when he is "too troubled to speak."

"But doesn't singing require speaking?" someone asks. And the answer reminds us of the strange power of song.

Basically, song comes from a different reservoir than speech. Psychologists sometimes speak of music coming from "the right brain." Of course, not that there are two brains, but that while singing, it's usually true that brain wave activity goes on in the right hemisphere of the brain, while reasoned speech is more naturally located in the left hemisphere.

Now it's one of God's greatest blessings that the right hemisphere of the brain is also the seat of much of our emotions, and not all of those emotions are upbeat all the time. How gracious for God to locate a soothing balm for sorrow such as song right alongside our sadness, as well as our joy. So the psalmist can also affirm, both that, "The Lord will command His lovingkindness in the daytime, and in the night His song shall be with me—a prayer to the God of my life" (Ps. 42:8).

Secular music has many examples of singing against the night. An entire musical style, "the blues," is popular among many people because of its power to face sadness with song—to avoid the temptation to deny that we're "down." "Blues" run that mood through the grid of music, which has the mysterious power to strain out the sadness and leave us somehow feeling better. As the secular tune "Song Sung Blue" reminds us, putting our sorrows into song often enables us to sing them right out again.

This is a part of the power of music at funerals. Ironically a noble "funeral dirge" doesn't always increase the sadness; it sometimes has the power to comfort, and to heal. This is the wisdom of some Christians who have congregational singing at funerals; it's a time for everyone who has experienced the loss, not just the organist or the special singers, to express themselves musically.

A final word about singing and sadness: it's a resource for the person who is grieving, not a Band-Aid for someone else to apply. Proverbs 25:20 says wisely, "Like one who takes away a garment in cold weather, and like vinegar on soda, is one who sings songs to a heavy heart." In other words, the advice, "Cheer up and sing!" doesn't usually help. Rather, the ability to sing against the night is something for the individual to receive as a gift from the One who gives us songs in the night.

Praise in Prayer

We praise You our Father for being a God who has the power to give us a song, not just when we feel like singing, but even in the dark nights of the soul. Help us to sing in tune with You, Amen.

Selected Readings

| 1 Samuel 12:16-23 | Isaiah 35:1-10 |
| Psalm 18:1-6 | Jeremiah 31:10-13 |

Praise in Practice

1. Share an experience that illustrates the point of this chapter—one when singing even a sad song brought cheer.

2. Is it difficult for you to sing and praise God when you are "down"?

18

Go Ahead and Dance!

"Praise Him with the sound of the trumpet; praise Him with the lute and harp! Praise Him with the timbrel and dance;... Let everything that has breath praise the Lord."—Psalm 150:3,4,6

When you really think about the majesty and goodness and power of God, your entire being seems to want to get in on the fun of praise. The entire material creation joins the chorus—musical instruments here, the rocks and the hills in other passages. Then there's that business about praising God with the dance—and many people balk there.

While some Christians are uninhibited enough to "dance in the aisles," many others associate dancing with worldliness, not spirituality. And of course it's easy to show that some dancing is suggestive and hardly fit for the glad-but-holy activity of worship. Others suppose it to be an overly emotional display.

But before dismissing dancing before the Lord as excess exuberance, we should recall the attitude of

Michal, David's wife, toward her husband's dancing in praise. You may recall that Israel's enemies, the Philistines, had captured the Ark of God—the center-piece of Israel's worship that contained mementos of their journey from Egypt. Both Israel and the Philistines had reduced the Ark to a kind of magical talisman, thinking that its mere presence in battle would ensure victory, and that without it they would be defeated.

At any rate, the Ark was sacred, and you can imagine the joy of King David and the people when it was recaptured from the Philistines. They set the precious symbol of God's presence among them on a new cart, and there was feasting and celebrating as they brought it back to Jerusalem. David and the people shouted with joy and trumpets—and then David removed his outer garment so he could move freely, and he "danced before the Lord with all his might" (2 Sam. 6:14).

Well, David's wife Michal felt just as some people do today. That was altogether too much of a display for her! "How glorious was the king of Israel today," she said sarcastically when he returned home, "uncovering himself today in the eyes of the maids of his servants, as one of the base fellows shamelessly uncovers himself!" Of course David wasn't "uncovered"—he wore an undergarment, a "linen ephod" (vs. 14). But when a person wants to be offended at something they're bound to find a reason. The truth is that Michal did not share David's ecstatic joy at the recovery of the Ark. She had a pouting spirit and a bitter heart, so she read negatives into David's abandon. To her it was at best an excessive display of emotionalism, and at worst immoral.

But God's Word evidences that He looked at the incident much differently. David was not ashamed to worship with passion. He wasn't turned aside from his pursuit of praise by what others might think. He was jubilant, joyous, childlike and humble in his praise. The psalms are like that. They are dynamic and expressive. They laugh and they weep. They lament and they praise, they reflect and emote. And they dance. They are a worship guide for whole persons.

So in the words of the song the gospel group "Dogwood" made popular many years ago, if the joy of the Lord penetrates you from head to toe, "Go Ahead and Dance!"

Praise in Prayer

Almighty God, help me to be so joyous and full of praise that at least my heart dances, celebrating Your majesty and love and making Your praise glorious. Let any presupposition that childlike praise is childish be humbled before You, Holy Father. Through Christ our Lord, Amen.

Selected Readings

1 Chronicles 15:25-29   Psalm 149:1-4
Psalm 30:8-12   Ecclesiastes 3:1-8

Praise in Practice

1. Now you suspected I might suggest that if praising

God in dance is foreign to you, you should try it, didn't you? If you are using this material in private devotion then there's no problem! Just choose an appropriate time and place; and if these devotionals are used in a group, share any feelings or thoughts you have about it.

2. How can you distinguish between dance that is pleasing to God, and that which incites wrong thoughts or immorality?

19

The Universe's Largest Choir

"They have seen Your procession, O God, the procession of my God, my King, into the sanctuary. The singers went before, the players on instruments followed after;...Bless God in the congregations, the Lord from the fountain of Israel."—Psalm 68:24-26

At its zenith Israelite worship must have been glorious, at times putting God's enemies in awe and disarray when they saw Israel's grand processions related to worshiping the true God. And the singing must have been especially inspiring. Here, special singers, a choir, actually, led the grand procession; but the congregation itself plays a central role in offering up praise to God.

It's important in today's Christian worship, too, that congregational participation not be diminished simply because the choir is specially trained and practiced to inspire our hearts. Choirs are not to substitute for us, but to stimulate our singing praise. In fact there is a sense in which all God's people themselves are the choir. In his vision of the end of time, the aged apostle John hears "as it were, the voice of a great multitude, as the sound of many waters and as the sound of mighty thunderings, saying 'Alleluia! For the Lord God Omnipotent reigns!'" (Rev. 19:6). Here is the universe's largest choir!

This reference to the central "role" played by the congregation in Israel's worship prompts our asking whether our public worship today is faithful to the congregational emphasis found in Scripture. We too easily make the choir, the minister and the worship or song leader the only actors in the drama of worship, and turn the congregation into an "audience." From this mistaken model, Sunday worship becomes a play "performed" before a Sunday morning audience, whose mission becomes criticizing performances, giving "thumbs up" or "thumbs down" reviews of the quality or ability of the "actors" in particular and the "show" in general.

Not at all! In true worship, God is the audience, and the cast is the whole assembled Body. The worship leaders aren't performing for the congregation; they are like directors whose responsibility is to enable the people to express effectively the "script" that essentially reads: "Make His praise glorious!" Of course they should be as skilled as possible, but worship isn't a "bomb" when a "performance" at the pulpit or on the stage or in the choir loft seems less effective by human tastes. Worship fails only when the people, the true "performers," fail to send up praise and glory and petition in humble adoration of the King before whom they have been called to give a "command performance."

In part, this is why private devotions are not sufficient for the Christian. As we have already noted, God "inhabit the praises of Israel"—the *gatherings* of His people (Ps. 22:3). The drama of worship is too grand a production to be produced by believers in lonely isolation from each other. So David worships on the hillsides, alone, but also says, "I will declare Your name to My brethren; in the midst of the congregation I will praise You" (22:22).

Just as the choir that leads the congregation in song is composed of multiple voices, so every one of the diverse gifts in the congregation is essential for acceptable worship. It is this individual gifting that the apostle Paul seizes on so effectively when he compares the church, the Lord's congregation, to a physical body in 1 Corinthians 12. Every member of the cast is important. You may not have been gifted as a soprano, alto, tenor or bass; but you are gifted, and your gift is needed in the universe's largest choir.

Praise in Prayer

Thank You, Lord, for the church—for believers with whom I can share life and faith in common. And when we assemble grant me a sense of personal participation with them in worship, instead of being a distant observer. In Jesus' name, Amen.

Selected Readings

Exodus 12:1-13   1 Corinthians 12:4-18
Leviticus 8:1-9   Hebrews 10:19-25

Praise in Practice

1. Why were "solidarity" and peoplehood especially important in the passage in Exodus, above?

2. Do you find heartfelt praise easier in private or in the assembly? Why?

20

The Power of Weakness Before the Awesome God

"O God, You are more awesome than Your
holy places. The God of Israel is He who gives
strength and power to His people."
—Psalm 68:35

I'm sure that if we knew more of the truth about the awesome God we would react something like Isaiah, whom we studied earlier. Return again to Isaiah 6, to this great scene that demonstrates the transforming power of standing before Him whom the psalmist calls "awesome." There is no more awe-inspiring scene in the Bible than this Throne room confrontation with the Thrice-Holy God.

Daunted by the pure holiness of God's dazzling robes, the strange creatures around His Throne, the shaking doorposts, and the echo of the cry, "Holy, holy, holy!", Isaiah seems melted—able only to say, "Woe is me!"

I doubt that the fullest worship of our hearts can occur without our understanding something of the overwhelmed anxiety one can imagine in Isaiah's voice. How else could anyone feel, standing in human imperfection before ultimate Perfectness? But in what has to be one of the most profound paradoxes in human experience, Isaiah emerges from the heavenly Throne room as a man of vision, direction, strength and mission.

We might say that he, a sinful man, was able to stand his ground in life only after being swept off his feet by God. And something like that should happen to us—to you, to me!—in worship. The trembling gives way to trust. We discover that His Supreme Power is to some extent transferable. It soon becomes apparent that our insufficiency is swallowed up in His all-sufficiency.

You see, God did not summon Isaiah to His Throne to scare the stamina out of him. God plays no games as a smoke-machine-pumping Wizard of Oz. Rather, God calls us to worship, and there He wants to display His might, because He knows we will face tasks in which we need to act mightily. He wants to supplant our unholiness with His holiness, our unwholeness with His wholeness. He is *not* disposed to *frighten us to death* for entering His presence, *but* to *awe us to life* because we have been in His presence. The Ground of All Being wants us to be able to stand our ground in life's trials. To do so in the face of sorrow, temptation, illness and disappointments requires frequent visits to the holy place. The God who is so much more awesome Himself than the appointments that awed Isaiah awaits there to fill us with a part of Himself.

Never hesitate to come to the awesome God, though coming in our weakness. Borrow from His divine strength, and then honor and praise the Source of our healing. Let's be taught by the parable of the Prodigal Son in Luke 15. Not only is the forgiving love of the Father taught there, but it's also about a son who, having flouted his regard for his father at first, later remembers and acknowledges the source of His security. Return to "home" was wonderful, but more awesome than the place was the person—his father. And he came to him...as we are invited to *the* Father.

Never believe you are too "down" and weak to still come to Him. Remember, He's waiting—God is waiting in the Throne room not to resist or dispel you, but to receive and reward you with strength sufficient for every tomorrow. Bring Him your fears and find new fearlessness in fearing Him. Bring Him your weakness and find strength in His might.

Praise in Prayer

Holy Father, I would not dare to come into Your presence without Your having called me to come, and without the covering of the blood of Jesus. I honor You and magnify Your Name, asking only that I may be strengthened by being in Your presence. Through Christ my Lord, Amen.

Selected Readings

Judges 13:8-23   Isaiah 66:1-2
Psalm 104:31-35   Hebrews 12:18-29

Praise in Practice

1. Was your earliest remembered awareness of God frightening or reassuring?

2. As a parent or Bible school teacher, plan how you can help youth under your influence grasp something of both the awesomeness of God and His willingness to strengthen us.

3. Do the assemblies where you worship foster a sense of the awesomeness and holiness of God? How is this best done?

21

What Language Shall I Borrow?

"Praise is awaiting You, O God, in Zion; and to You the vow shall be performed. O You who hear prayer, to You all flesh will come."
—Psalm 65:1,2

God has designed worship to fit every aspect of our nature. And, as we've noted, He wants us to employ every part of ourselves—body and soul, mind and spirit—in glorifying and worshiping Him. Let's focus on another aspect of worshiping God with the mind—specifically, the use of human speech in praising God.

Speech is one of the foremost gifts that distinguishes human beings from animals. Our capacity for the most common conversation or for the most learned discourse is a part of our having been created in the image of God. It is also a key to our exercising the dominion God has appointed mankind over the rest of His creation. The exercise of that responsible rule requires sensitive, and sensible communication. And it all flows most effectively out of our daily communication offered to God in worship and prayer.

In His wisdom, God has ordained several different kinds of prayer. If we think of the act of prayer as a fruit basket filled with a variety of lovely fruits we may bring to God as a gift, we will better see the idea in Hebrews 13:15's admonition: "By Him let us continually offer the sacrifice of praise to God, that is, the fruit of our lips, giving thanks to His name." Sample the variety:

First, let us approach God with the language or prayer of *confession*, acknowledging our sins and imperfection, and our longing to partake of His holiness.

Second, let us continue to offer the fruit of our lips with the language of *petition*. Here we recall that He has promised, "Ask, and it will be given to you" (Matt. 7:7). But we also petition God to understand what we are to do for Him, praying for insight into His will for us.

Third, with the language of *praise* He enables us to, "Enter into His gates with thanksgiving, and into His courts with praise" (Ps. 100:4). And we remain in His presence as we worship, recalling His goodness, His love and the grandeur of His being.

Fourth, *meditation* is also a part of our speech in God's presence. This form of prayer was never meant as some mystical way of "uniting with the universe," but has been given as a way of *waiting* upon God, knowing that just "being together" deepens our intimacy with Him.

94

Fifth and sixth, in prayer our speech also includes *intercession* and *supplication*. There's never a shortage of situations needing His intervention, so we intercede—being bold enough to ask Him to step in the middle of a muddle! Supplication is contracting with God to invade our present dilemma with His wisdom, power and provision.

Finally, our worshipful praying includes *exaltation* and *adoration*. We magnify Him who is worthy above all others and adore Him simply because of who He is.

Man uses the gift of speech for many purposes and in many ways. Because language is a function of the intellect, we have the choice between speaking in ways and words that glorify God, or in language that dishonors Him. Such prayer is our best exercise of our intelligence, which though limited at best, is still a mighty means to honor our Creator—with "the fruit of our lips."

Praise in Prayer

You know my prayers, O Lord, even before I put them into words. I praise You for the gift of language, and ask only that my speech, both in worship and in everyday life, will glorify You. Through Christ Jesus my Lord, Amen.

Selected Readings

Psalm 32:1-7	Matthew 6:5-15
Isaiah 38	Luke 18:9-14

Praise in Practice

1. Sing one or more of your favorite prayer-songs. Suggestions are "Dear Lord and Father of Mankind" (confession), and "Thou Art Worthy" (praise and exaltation).

2. Think of and share any experiences you have had with answered prayer.

3. What about unanswered prayer? What attitude should we have about prayers that seemingly go unanswered?

4. Which of the kinds of prayers in this chapter does God most often hear arising from your own private praying?

22

With Tongues of Men and of Angels

"O praise the Lord, all ye nations: praise him, all ye people. For his merciful kindness is great toward us: and the truth of the Lord endureth for ever. Praise ye the Lord."—Psalm 117 (*KJV*)

Biblical faith is a missionary faith. Even here in the Old Testament, the psalmist challenges "all ye nations" (or Gentiles, *NKJV*) to praise the Lord. But it remained for the early Christians to really get serious about missionary work. It started at the church's very beginning. A miracle occurred that proclaimed the praises of God in various languages confirming God's interest in the nations they represented.

The story is told in Acts 2: the scene, the birthday of the Church, and the time was the first Pentecost feast after the resurrection of Christ. The disciples were waiting in Jerusalem in obedience to Christ's command:

"Tarry in the city of Jerusalem until you are endued with power from on high" (Luke 24:49). Why Jerusalem? Because it was God's plan that, "repentance and remission of sins should be preached in His name to all nations, beginning at Jerusalem" (vs. 47). Here, then, is the fulfillment of the psalmist's reference to "the nations" (or Gentiles) praising the Lord in Psalm 117.

In God's providence, the feast day had brought to Jerusalem visitors "from every nation under heaven." Suddenly, the Holy Spirit descended with a sound "as of a rushing mighty wind" (Acts 2:2). Tongues of fire, demonstrating the Holy Spirit's holy presence, appeared above the disciples' heads, and they "began to speak with other tongues, as the Spirit gave them utterance" (vs. 4).

We can only imagine the stunning impact of all these visitors from so many nations hearing these linguistically unschooled Jews speak in their own foreign languages (see Acts 2:5-13). Of course if you were from Ethiopia and you heard someone speaking in the language of Gaul it might be unintelligible; and sure enough, some in the crowd mocked, accusing the speakers of having feasted on too much wine. But the apostle Peter stood up and explained from the prophets that the sign of "tongues" was a direct fulfillment of prophecy.

The early church continued in this supernatural gift, both in earthly languages they'd never studied ("tongues of men") and possibly, according to Paul, even in heavenly utterances—("tongues...of angels"—1 Cor. 13:1). The apostle gave clear instructions on the use of these gifts in the church, whether in prophesying, prayer or edification (1 Cor. 14).

Why would anyone want to deny the church today such a wonderful gift of praise, prayer or benediction? In the privacy of my room I can quietly give my tongue over to the Holy Spirit as I praise God in a prayer language He gives me. And in the gathered congregation we can give utterance by the same movement of the Spirit, whether in prayer, or a word of prophecy, or edification or a sign to unbelievers as this gift is interpreted by its matching gift (1 Cor. 14:14-22).

What a glorious cosmic concert! The various melodies of earth's differing languages all blending in the power of the Spirit, into a chorus in which both people and angels lift their voices to glorify the Giver of every good gift.

Praise in Prayer

Father, I praise You that Your Name is being praised in loving and supernatural ways around the globe today where people of every race and tongue have heard and received the Good News. Please use me in whatever way my tongue can best be used to glorify You and to speak the truth in love and to release ever-new praises to Your Name. Through Jesus, my wonderful Lord, Amen.

Selected Readings

Joel 2:28-32   1 Corinthians 12:1-11
Acts 2:14-39   1 Corinthians 14:6-19

Praise in Practice

1. Have you been given a prayer language or other indication of the present-day gift of tongues? If so, how would you describe it, and what would you say to a fellow-believer who would like to praise God in this way, but never has?

2. What caution does the apostle Paul raise for those with the gift of tongues in 1 Corinthians 13:1?

3. If you haven't experienced this gift, what word do you hear from Paul in 1 Corinthians 12:12-31? On the other hand, do you resist this gift? Why or why not?

4. Have you experienced situations when the gift of tongues was divisive? How does 1 Corinthians 12:20-25 speak to this issue?

23

New Songs for Renewed People

"Rejoice in the Lord, O you righteous! For praise from the upright is beautiful. Praise the Lord with the harp; make melody to Him with an instrument of ten strings. Sing to Him a new song; play skillfully with a shout of joy."
—Psalm 33:1-3

Several years ago, when my grandson Kyle was just beginning to talk, his mother, our oldest daughter, was teaching him to pray. He had already learned to bow his head when others prayed, but this day he was assured that "this will be your very own prayer." Now, before continuing the story, you need also to know that Kyle was an enthusiastic viewer of the children's TV program "Sesame Street." His favorite character on the show was "Count Count," and he was learning his numbers from the way the Count says them; very slowly, dramatically, pausing after each one—"Ah, one...Ah, two...Ah, three..." and so forth—adding a "ha-ha-ha" in traditional Count Count fashion.

So, it was in that context the little guy was listening when his mother said, "Say what I say," and then proceeded into the prayer. "Dear Father...," she said.

The infant dutifully said something like, "D'Fahr."

"Thank you..." said his mother.

"T'kyu," came the echo.

Then, "for...." But here the just-two-year-old thought she said, *four*, and mistaking it as a Count Count cue, triumphantly shouted "FIVE! Ha-ha-ha!"

Well, it's a laughable mistake, but how it illustrates our human ability to mix up former things we've learned from God with new things being given His children, His church; things that impact our own distinctive worship patterns. In the last decade, a most dramatic development has been an ever-widening expansion of powerful worship and praise through music; worship that contains the newness mentioned in our text. This awakening isn't just the result of new talent, though leadership is always a part of renewal. But it's as though the Body of Christ at large has sensed the power of music to both magnify God *and* rise up against the powers of spiritual darkness. And I can only say, "Hallelujah!"

This stirring in the Church is deeply rooted in Scripture—especially illustrated in the renewal of worship under King David in the Old Testament. In 1 Chronicles 25:1, David and his leaders appointed "some of the sons of Asaph, of Heman, and of Jeduthun, who should prophesy with harps, stringed instruments, and cymbals." These servants "were under the direction of Asaph, who prophesied according to the order of the king" (vs. 2).

What a significant moment in the glorious story of God's people at worship! May God give us today servants like those, who will "prophesy"—communicate the Spirit's timeless message—in songs and hymns, and with a variety of instruments skillfully played. God give them a spirit of obedience and service so they are communicating no other message than His Word! God help our assemblies to ring with the sound and voice of the old message in new songs for a new era in the Church!

Make no mistake: Satan will be vanquished from any congregation whose music and song is renewed in the power of the Spirit to provide marching music for the Kingdom of God!

Praise in Prayer

Praise to You, O Lord, for the musical gifts You have given Your church. Help our song to glorify Your Name. Help our music to be an accompaniment to the furthering of Your Word. Through Jesus we pray, Amen.

Selected Readings

1 Chronicles 25:1-8 Psalm 98
Psalm 40:1-3 Revelation 14:1-5

Praise in Practice

1. What part of the church's music helps you praise God most effectively? (Choral? Orchestra or band? Singing groups or solos?)

2. Do you think worship would be enhanced if the church offered instruction in singing, or should it flow naturally from those with natural ability?

24
Worship and the Word

"Oh, that my ways were directed to keep Your statutes! Then I would not be ashamed, when I look into all Your commandments....I will keep Your statutes."—Psalm 119:5,6,8

It is impossible to worship God acceptably and not come to Him in right relationship to His statutes—the Word of God. It is folly to suppose that we can come to Him "in the Spirit" if in our own spirits there is a tendency to neglect commitment to actually doing what the Bible says.

Much of the book of Hebrews compares and contrasts our relationship to God under the New Covenant with Israel's relationship to Him under the Old. Again and again the Hebrew writer refers to God's requirement to pattern the Tabernacle—that great temple-in-the-wilderness—and its appointments precisely according to His Word through Moses. In Hebrews, there is always this sobering sense of, "If it was that way then, how much more so now...."

Yet, however sincerely we relate to the Word of God, we seem always to do so imperfectly. None of us knows it all, nor are we able to plumb the Word's depths and come up with precisely the right understanding of every facet of its truth. So what are we to do?

The answer is to stay with the Hebrew writer, and allow him to explain how Christ has already built the perfect tabernacle for us. "Christ came as High Priest of the good things to come, with the greater and more perfect tabernacle not made with hands,...Not with the blood of goats and calves, but with His own blood He entered the Most Holy Place once for all, having obtained eternal redemption" (Heb. 9:11,12).

This does not dismiss us from our responsibility to obey His Word of the New Covenant. It simply means that it is through the sufficiency of Jesus, not through our ability to know Scripture perfectly, that we are now able to stand in right relationship to His Word. Christ in fact creates in the genuine worshiper a spirit of willingness to follow His Word as it is revealed to him.

How often I've heard some people say, when first hearing or seeing God being worshiped in the Spirit as His Word describes, "Well, that's just not my style." Beloved, the idea is that when you and I come to God He transforms us—changes us—into *His* style. You did know, didn't you, when you came to Him, that transformation is what it's all about...that you can't come into the presence of the living God without being changed? We don't just "flake it" in the name of the Spirit! We *grow,* we *learn,* we are *shaped* by the power of the Word, which has been given by the Holy Spirit (see 2 Pet. 1:19-21).

True worship is never separate from the Word. We hear the Word of grace that comes to us as coals from the altar on which Christ gave Himself for us, burning away our misunderstandings and inadequate knowledge. And hearing that Word of forgiveness for our sin and failures not only makes us want all the more to worship and praise Him, but to say, "Speak, Lord, Your servant is listening. Command, and I will obey."

Praise in Prayer

We praise You, dear Father, not just for the way worship can cause our spirits to soar, but for Your Word also, which tells us what our lives and our worship should be. Help us to connect with You in our understanding of the Word, and in our times of praise. Through Christ our Lord, Amen.

Selected Readings

1 Samuel 15:10-22	Hebrews 4:11-16
Psalm 119:9-16	Hebrews 8:1-13

Praise in Practice

1. Do you feel any conflict between the "rational" task of Bible study—really digging deeply into the Word—and the "emotional" experience of praising and

worshiping in the Spirit? Discuss the similarities and differences.

2. How can following the moral and ethical principles in the Word in daily life be occasions of praise and worship to God?

3. In 1 Samuel 15:10-22 (see the Selected Readings, above), what was wrong with King Saul's attempt to offer sacrifices in worship to God?

4. How can we know that the Holy Spirit will not tell us to do anything that is in violation of Scripture?

25

Praise: The Weapon of Our Warfare

"Your hand will find all Your enemies; Your right hand will find those who hate You....Be exalted, O Lord, in Your own strength! We will sing and praise Your power."—Psalm 21:8,13

Some people have trouble with passages in the Psalms that pray for God to deal violently with the enemies of His people. While there is a difference between some Old Testament attitudes and the teaching of Christ to "love your enemies," the Psalms are not totally vengeful and vindictive. In general, the Old Testament makes a distinction between taking revenge ourselves, and leaving our enemies to God. Strength and power lie in Him, not ourselves, as this psalm confesses.

The role of praise in dealing with our enemies is also strange, to many people. There are many good reasons for glorifying and worshiping God—His sheer magnitude and magnificence, the fact that He is our Redeemer, that He commanded us to praise Him, and that praise is healthy and healing to the whole person—these are some good reasons. But the psalmist also praises God in the midst of facing adversity at the hand of an enemy. Do you wonder how such conflict and praise meet?

The relationship is explained from a human standpoint in what is one of the strangest stories in the history of warfare. It's in 2 Chronicles 20, where King Jehoshaphat and the Kingdom of Judah are about to be attacked by a horde far outnumbering them. You might compare their plight to a situation of your own when everything seems to go wrong, or when the force of Satan's opposition threaten to overpower you. King Jehoshaphat's experience offers a way to do battle in such situations. It begins by simply confessing, "We have no power against this great multitude" (2 Chron. 20:12).

But that confession of weakness didn't mean that Judah did nothing—nor should we. A prophet of Judah delivered a word from the Lord, God saying that the battle was His, not theirs. For their response, the people "stood up to praise the Lord God of Israel with voices loud and high" (vs. 19). Then, instead of hurling spears or boulders, the army marched out boldly hurling phrases of praises, singing "Praise the Lord, for His mercy endures forever" (vs. 21). The result? The Lord Himself set ambushes for the enemy and caused confusion and fighting to break out among themselves. There was an utter rout!

So what attack should believers mount against Satan

and his hordes? We are to take up the weapons we wield best—the weapons of praise. As the apostle Paul taught, "the weapons of our warfare are not carnal but mighty in God for pulling down strongholds" (2 Cor. 10:4).

Faced with the forces of evil, God's people are not to fear. Our greatest resource of resistance doesn't arise from any arsenal known to human wisdom or device. It comes from knowing that the battle is the Lord's. We are never to react from a position of weakness, but to act from one of strength. That strength is found in faithfully remaining at our post of praise. Our best defense is to do what we should know how to do best: Offer praise and glory to the Living God, whose enemies will always finally flee before His might and power.

Praise in Prayer

You know my human weaknesses, O God. You know that I live in a world where the strength of praise is scoffed at as weakness. Catch me up in the realm of spiritual truth, so that in difficulty I may remain at my post of praise. Through Jesus Christ, my victorious Lord, Amen.

Selected Readings

2 Chronicles 20:22-30   Isaiah 31:1-3
Psalm 147:1-11   Revelation 19:1-7

Praise in Practice

1. What is your first reaction likely to be when someone attacks you, either verbally or physically? Does praising the Lord as a line of defense seem to be totally unrealistic?

2. On a 3×5 card, write words such as, "The weapon of His people is praise." Carry the card with you in your pocket or purse for a couple of days, taking it out and reading it frequently to refresh your memory. Discuss with a friend whether this exercise helped impress the truth of today's reflection on your mind.

26

The Power of Praise in Evangelism

"Restore to me the joy of Your salvation, and uphold me with Your generous Spirit. Then I will teach transgressors Your ways, and sinners shall be converted to You."
—Psalm 51:12,13

It was midnight. Two Christians with a seemingly lost cause sat in the darkness of a prison. Paul and Silas have been jailed in the city of Philippi for preaching Christ. It would have been so easy for them to sink down on the floor of their cell and ask, "Why me, Lord?" But what do they do? They pray and sing hymns, filling the night with their song of praise to God.

You remember the result, which was nothing short of amazing. There was a mighty earthquake and the doors of the prison sprang open. The jailor called for a light, and seeing the open cell doors would have taken his own life. But Paul reassured him that no prisoner had escaped. The jailor was so awed by it all that he asked for salvation and was converted that very night (Acts 16:25-34).

God impressed this passage of Scripture on our minds at one of our first meetings at The Church On The Way. Ten years later we looked back and marveled at God's grace—from twenty-four people, including Anna, me and our four children, to the thousands who had been brought to the Lord. Since we had not launched any elaborate evangelistic programs, what caused this growth? I am convinced it was because God taught us a path of evangelism through our commitment to worship. We learned how, in the words of Psalm 51, that through God's gift of joy and a spirit of praise in our assemblies, "many transgressors" found the way of the Lord through those gatherings.

"Look outside your walls," God was saying to us. "Look at the people who are in darkness, just like the Philippian jailor. They are in prison, but I will send an earthquake! They don't know the psalm of praise, but I will teach you the psalm, and as you lift your voices many beyond these walls will hear and, as with the jailor, it will become for them a song of deliverance!"

By now you know that these personal references never intend to suggest there was anything we did in our own strength at our church. Neither am I downplaying the importance of assertive, overt evangelism— of witnessing, reaching everyone we can with the Good News of grace—even confronting them with the claims of the Lord Jesus on their lives. Nor am I discounting the importance of strong pulpit proclamation, or the role of the Sunday School in evangelism.

What I am saying is that when we as God's people learn to center on the core of our reason for being, we'll be found faithful in worship, and a mighty release of *life* ensues. Evangelistic results will increase, not through the attraction of a Christian superstar or due to highly studied and programmed techniques of soul-winning, but through the message of "joy" the psalmist mentions in worship. We are faced here with a simple spiritual law. When God's people focus on their primary business of praise and worship, the situation becomes shot through with power. They simply can't help but become God's magnet, drawing people from darkness into light.

Praise in Prayer

Dear Father, help my worship and devotion to be a beacon to those in darkness, a light that cannot be hidden under a bushel, a city set on a hill. Especially bless our fellowship of believers with a vision of praising You so faithfully that it frees those who dwell in darkness. In Jesus' name, Amen.

Selected Readings

Psalm 148:7-14	Daniel 3:8-18
Isaiah 42:1-12	1 Peter 3:1-4

Praise in Practice

1. What first attracted you to the Lord? Was it in any way connected with a congregation whose praise and worship made you want to become a part of a worshiping community?

2. Of what value are organized evangelistic campaigns? Should they be specifically related to local churches, or is it enough to introduce people to Jesus?

3. Read Paul's teaching on tongues as a sign "to unbelievers" (1 Cor. 14:22-25). Explain in your own words the meaning of this passage, verse by verse.

27

Praise and the New Creation

"O Lord, how manifold are Your works! In wisdom You have made them all....You send forth Your Spirit, they are created; and You renew the face of the earth."—Psalm 104:24,30

We were gathered for a retreat in a beautiful setting that impressed us all with God's power as expressed in creation. The wind was blowing through the trees, and, recalling that the Hebrew word for wind also means "spirit," it seemed that the Spirit of God was telling us something about another creation. He seemed to be saying, "I want you to be equally impressed with the New Creation that I can bring about when you allow the wind of My Spirit to breathe through to branches of your lives. Your psalm of praise will become an accompaniment to My creative works, and hearts will be changed, lives turned around and sins forgiven."

How thrilling to be a part of an expanding creation. Even in the physical world, science speaks of the universe expanding at a speed that approaches the speed of light. God had only to say the word, "Let there be!" and creation not only happened, but continues to occur with blinding speed. And the Bible says that God does all this to the music of praise!

In Job 38, God is chiding Job for his presumption: "Where were you when I laid the foundations of the earth?" He asks, "When the morning stars sang together, and all the sons of God shouted for joy?" (vs. 4,7). This is an apparent reference to the angels of God looking on in awe as worlds were flung into existence. They formed a heavenly choir singing in exultation and amazement. "Look at that!" they must have shouted, "Praise God!" And in the psalmist's words, "How manifold are Your works!"

Since God does His creative work against a background of angelic praise, it seems an awesome responsibility and privilege is before us as we seek to see God continue to expand His works in the spiritual world around us. For example, those who come to Christ are called a "new creation" (2 Cor. 5:17). When sinners turn to the Lord, when the sorrowful are made joyful in the Lord, it is a fulfillment of the psalmist's prediction: "This will be written for the generation to come, that a people *yet to be created* may praise the Lord" (Ps. 102:18, emphasis mine). Believe it, loved one. God is at work, to the tune of Christians like you and me who are tending to our joyful task of praise and worship, saying, "Look at that! Praise God!" Let's let our voices join those of the angels again, who rejoice over one sinner who repents (see Luke 15:7,10).

All of us are vulnerable to becoming people who only stand up when the worship leader says to stand, sing when told to sing, and maybe say, "Praise the Lord" in a perfunctory way, not really sensing that something real is waiting to happen. Beloved, once we catch the vision of the continuing creation in which God is engaged, and how He awaits worshipers who will create a backdrop of praise against which His divine power may be manifested, we will never worship passively again. There is no limit. Creation is ongoing. There are people to be converted, hearts to be enlightened, eyes to be opened, people to be healed! And God is looking for a chorus to provide the accompaniment!

Praise in Prayer

Be exalted, O God our Creator! For You have spun creation into motion, and we glorify You for its marvels and majesty. Help our praise to form a fitting chorus to accompany Your continuing creative power in the lives of people. Through Christ, the Instrument of Your creation, Amen.

Selected Readings

Job 38:1-18	Luke 15:11-32
Psalm 33:6-15	2 Corinthians 5:14-21

Praise in Practice

1. What is the most magnificent part of God's "natural" creation to you—the aspect of creation that brings to mind most forcefully God's majesty and power?

2. What similarities and differences can you think of between the material creation and "new creations in Christ"? Does the element of free will in people coming to the Lord make these "creations" even more glorious?

3. Have you ever known people to be moved to respond to Christ at an evangelistic service as a result of a moving service of praise and worship?

28

The Lord's Beauty Salon

"Praise the Lord! For it is good to sing praises to our God; for it is pleasant, and praise is beautiful."—Psalm 147:1

I have often said that if you want to become a handsome or a beautiful person, praise the Lord! You may know people who have lived in the presence of the Lord so long, and who love Him so much, they begin to prove the truth of this psalm, "praise is beautiful." Their very demeanor speaks of "the beauty of holiness," and their countenance evidences the beautifying power of praise.

Do you remember our words in the introduction to these studies; comments about our becoming more and more like the being we worship? This clearly is an important principle to our Father, because twice He says, both in Psalm 115:8 and 135:18, that those who worship idols "are like them." But the same is true of we who steadfastly look into the face of the Lord until His countenance begins to be mirrored in ours: His grace fashioning us into gracious people, His beauty transforming our own countenances.

Now, "beauty" may not be your first thought when you get up in the morning and stare into the mirror. Stress, tragedy or deep sorrow may have etched creases of weariness or suffering into your face. But make this experiment: prove God's Word. Take that countenance, as it is, into the presence of the Lord day after day, in frequent, steadfast praise and worship. The prophet Isaiah says plainly what you will receive, in return. He promises that the Servant of the Lord, the One who turned out to be the Messiah, is sent specifically "to console those who mourn in Zion, to give them beauty for ashes, the oil of joy for mourning" (Isa. 61:3). That's an oil that surpasses any temporal "youthening" effect of human cosmetics!

In Bible times, ashes were a sign of grief and mourning. When Tamar was defiled by her brother Absalom, she put ashes on her head and tore her robe in anguish (2 Sam. 13:19). Job sat in ashes as a sign of his desperate plight (Job. 2:8), and when God confronted him, Job said, "I abhor myself, and repent in dust and ashes" (42:6). Ashes could signify deep humility or even insignificance. When Abraham dared to intercede in behalf of the wicked city of Sodom, he said to God, "I who am but dust and ashes have taken it upon myself to speak to the Lord" (Gen. 18:27).

Now comes the promised Servant predicted by Isaiah—Jesus the Lord! He sees people in ashes, people uncertain about God, devoid of hope, oppressed by the realization of their own imperfection and weakness. What a desolate picture...how unlovely we *all* are without the Messiah! But, whisper it expectantly; *but* His love and mercy offer the perfect sin offering on the altar of God, and from the ashes of His offering a marvelous transformation affects the souls *and the faces* of those who accept it. The inner beauty of Christ Himself begins to shine. Forgiven, their pinched and anguished faces relax in God's peace. Loved, their countenances glow. Caught up in praise, they worship in "the beauty of holiness." In the world's most marvelous miracle, they—indeed, *we!*—have been given beauty in the place of ashes.

Praise in Prayer

Beautiful Savior, I love to gaze upon You, and to feel Your love becoming a part of who I am. I honor You above all beautiful things in heaven and on earth, just for who You are, and for Your power to touch even sordid lives and transform them into beautiful people. We praise You in Jesus' name, Amen.

Selected Readings

Psalm 48   Isaiah 4:2-6
Psalm 102:1-11   Isaiah 61:1-11

1. Describe someone you know, perhaps an older person, who seems to have an inner beauty that comes from knowing and worshiping the Lord.

2. Many people can recall the old saying many parents have said to a daughter: "Pretty is as pretty does." Does this also express a Christian truth?

3. Do you think there is too much emphasis on external beauty in our society? In the church?

4. What traits do you think best describe a spiritually beautiful person?

29

Jewels in the Treasury of the Lord

"Praise the Lord! Praise the name of the Lord;
Praise Him, O you servants of the Lord! You
who stand in the house of the Lord,...sing
praises to His name, for it is pleasant. For the
Lord has chosen Jacob for Himself, Israel for
His special treasure."—Psalm 135:1-4

Let's admit it. Some people in our gatherings for praise and worship don't always share the psalmist's sentiment that praise is "pleasant." They seem frozen, at best only singing because someone said to. Perhaps they are pre-occupied with problems they bring into the assembly. Perhaps their church attendance has degenerated to a dull routine or ritualistic habit. Or perhaps their senses have just been so jaded and numbed by our media-dominated culture that they would find the combination of a space launch, a volcanic eruption and a three-ring circus dull and boring.

What difference does it make, anyway? such may think; *what good does praise do anyway?* But the Hebrew writer answers, speaking of praise in terms which declare the *fruit*-begetting power of praise: "By Him let us continually offer the sacrifice of praise to God, that is, the fruit of our lips, giving thanks to His name" (Heb. 13:15). What kind of fruit does he mean? If apples spilled from our lips, would it get our attention? How *much* do our words of praise count?

The prophet Malachi spoke to this issue. He addressed a people who said just what we've been describing: "It is vain to serve God" (Mal. 3:14). In confronting them, God added a wonderful promise, noting a coming day when believers will see that their service and worship was not in vain: "They shall be mine, saith the Lord of hosts, in that day when I make up my jewels" (vs. 17, *KJV*).

There is the "fruit" of which Hebrews 13:15 speaks. God's Word says there will come a day when you and I will see convincing evidence that our words of praise weren't lost in the air. They are even now being stored up in God's treasury. On that day God will bring out a treasure chest and say, "Look! These jewels, this treasure, is gathered from the words of praise you offered me while you were on earth. Well done—enter thou into the joys of your Lord!"

What further evidence could we require that praise "counts"? It isn't farfetched to say there are diamonds spilling from your lips with your words of worship. Just as with finances that we offer to God when we thought we couldn't afford the sacrifice. This is "bread" cast upon the water that will surely return. God does not forget such sacrifices, and the same is true of the sacrifice of praise that is the fruit of our lips. Never forsake *living* praise, mouthing rote sayings because someone else does. "The Lord has chosen Jacob,"—that's us, the spiritual "Israel"—for His treasure. And the praise that arises from our lips is real, lasting and being gathered in a treasury of priceless jewels that I'm convinced we'll all see when we meet our Lord in glory!

Praise in Prayer

Let my lips avoid vain repetition as I lift my voice in praise, O Lord. Distract me from distractions, awaken me from dullness of mind, and transform habit and routine into vibrant times of worship. Grant me a vision of the jewels of praise You are gathering as the fruit of my lips. Through Jesus Christ my Lord, Amen.

Selected Readings

Psalm 19:7-11   Jeremiah 31:10-16
Isaiah 62   Hebrews 11:1-6

Praise in Practice

1. If your thoughts ever have a tendency to wander during worship times, share why you think this is, and what individual worshipers can do to focus, and make their worship truly meaningful.

2. What can be done by the church and its leaders as a Body to conduct services that are conducive to meaningful praise times?

3. Is it appropriate to think of praise, and of any other aspect of living in obedience to God, as having a reward, or is that an unworthy idea? Is there a difference between reward as a natural consequence and fulfillment of God's promise, and as the primary motive for serving God?

30

Enter His Courts with an Offering, Too

"Give to the Lord, O kindreds of the peoples, give to the Lord glory and strength. Give to the Lord the glory due His name; bring an offering, and come into His courts."—Psalm 96:7,8

It is impossible to talk about worship in a biblical framework without talking about offering to God our material substance—our money. This isn't because He needs our wealth, any more than He needs us to feed His ego with our praise. But the fact is, giving our financial resources is a proper response that opens the way to functioning in the fundamental spiritual law of giving and receiving. *Giving* generously is the measure of how generously we can *receive*—how open we are to the inpouring of God's blessing.

The apostle Paul taught this to the Corinthians when he reminded them of the financial gifts he was soliciting for the impoverished, famine-ridden saints in Judea: "But this I say: He who sows sparingly will also reap sparingly, and he who sows bountifully will also reap bountifully" (2 Cor. 9:6). You see, God wants to pour into our lives His blessings, but our capacity to receive them depends on whether we "let out the plug" at the giving end of our lives. God created us to be channels of blessing, but our ability to receive the resources with which He wants us to bless others, depends on our being able to give them away—freely, faithfully, generously. Here's the process: (1) He provides, (2) we trust and give, (3) He blesses our gifts to others, then (4) He fills us again with His abundant provision.

King David understood this principle well. When God commanded him to make a special sacrifice, David chose for a location the nearby threshing floor of Ornan the Jebusite. When David asked Ornan how much the site was worth, Ornan protested that he wanted to give it to the king for nothing—along with the oxen for the burnt offering, and the threshing implements for the firewood. But knowing the law of giving and receiving, David replied, "No, but I will surely buy it for the full price, for I will not take what is yours for the Lord, nor offer burnt offerings with that which costs me nothing" (1 Chron. 21:24).

At times, the Israelites proved the validity of this law in a negative way. During a time when they were feeling the absence of God, the prophet Malachi explained the problem to them. It was their shallow neglect of giving which blocked their way. They had been robbing God of tithes and offerings. God prescribed the remedy:

"Bring all the tithes into the storehouse...[and see] if I will not open for you the windows of heaven and pour out for you such blessing that there will not be room enough to receive it" (Mal. 3:10).

Again, God summons our tithes as a part of praise-filled worship, not because He is out of money, nor even essentially because Christian work requires our funds. But our tithes are *first* a token of how much we truly honor Him with praising hearts and lives. Offerings given to God are a gauge of whether we can be commended like the churches of Macedonia, who "first gave *themselves* to the Lord" (2 Cor. 8:1-5, emphasis mine).

God's intended blessings of material resources are far more abundant than we can imagine or can ever repay. Let praiseful, obedient giving break any "free-loading" spirit, and according to His generosity and grace let us worship with abounding financial gifts of our gratitude.

Praise in Prayer

God of good and gracious gifts, I praise You for blessing me with so many good things. Increase my capacity to be content with what I receive, and as You help me become a generous giver, make me an example of one You can trust to give aboundingly as You increase my ability to praise You in this way. Through Him who gave His all for me, Amen.

Selected Readings

1 Chronicles 21:18-27   Matthew 6:25-34
Malachi 3:1-12   2 Corinthians 9:6-15

Praise in Practice

1. Many Christians can bear witness to the way God responds to sacrifice with an outpouring of blessings. Share any such experience, not as boasting of your sacrificial giving but to encourage others to believe God's promise to bless those who "seek first the kingdom."

2. Determine to pause sometime during each day for a week to consciously focus on God's good gifts. Breathe in deeply as you praise God for His blessings; breathe out fully as you determine to pass along His gifts to others.

3. Make a study of tithing, with the help of a concordance or Bible dictionary. Is it just an Old Testament ordinance, or does it apply to Christians?

31

Worship and the Meaning of Life

---

*"All our days have passed away in Your wrath;
we finish our years like a sigh. The days of our
lives are seventy years; and if by reason of
strength they are eighty years, yet their boast is
only labor and sorrow; for it is soon cut off,
and we fly away,...So teach us to number our
days, that we may gain a heart of wisdom."*
—Psalm 90:9,10,12

We are only faithful to the book of Psalms when we
consider their balance. It's a praise book for all seasons: when we rejoice in the Lord and exult over His
providential care, and when our souls nearly burst with
pain in times of darkness.

What can we do when life seems hard, defeating,
unfulfilling and aimless? Well, we can be honest in our
prayers, as the psalmist was. We can cry to God, as in

Psalm 90:13, "Return, O Lord! How long? And have compassion on Your servants."

Can you see what is happening here? This writer isn't crying out in dark unbelief, but in the light of hope. In short, he is *worshiping*. The fact his heart isn't overflowing with blessing or abundance is no hindrance to his worship. For this one, it becomes all the more reason to seek solace and refuge in God. We'd never find this one staying home from the praise assembly muttering, "I don't feel like worshiping"!

The psalmist was wise enough to know that as Bible translator J. B. Phillips put it, there's "A God-shaped hole that only He can fill." Or as Augustine said, "You have made us for Yourself, and our hearts find no rest until they find it in You."

Even in the dark times, we must realize the vast power of worship to give our lives meaning and purpose. For one thing, bowing before any god *declares our values*. If we surrender to the lying deity veiled in feelings of despair and aimlessness when they visit us, we will bow before hopelessness exchanging the Almighty God for a lesser god. But worshiping God even amid despair is a way to defy the Adversary and declare our valuing of the good—the best—in life: The Lord! There is no more worthy purpose to praise; no more worthy time for it!

In worship we also *name priorities*. Putting God first enables us to focus on first things—His love, our blessings, our responsibility to others—instead of the temporary feelings of despair. Worship sets the priority of who you look to for guidance. It even forms certain expectations, so that our worship determines what we will yet discover in our future.

And worship is a way of *setting goals*, removing the sense that we're not going anywhere. Just the act of acknowledging that *God*, not the darkness, holds our future can enable us to "number our days"—to entrust our way to Him even when it's too dark to see our next step.

The despairing moment in which the psalmist wrote this text eventually passed. He overcame, insisting on remaining in God's presence, even when the temple was dark and he could not see the way. Even so, in our own times of confusion and aimlessness, remembering the power of worshiping in the darkness will enable us to order our days aright, and to finish them—not with a sigh but a shout!

Praise in Prayer

Dear Lord, as I come before You, I confess that without You life is meaningless. Grant me, as I praise You, a vision of who I am, and what I am to do. Help me to order my days in ways that glorify Your name, and even when I cannot see my way, to trust Your providence. Through Jesus my Lord, Amen.

Selected Readings

Psalm 80:1-7	Ecclesiastes 12:1-7,13
Psalm 90:11-17	Ephesians 5:8-21

Praise in Practice

1. In what specific ways does your faith give meaning and purpose to your life? It may be helpful to group them in the categories this devotional suggests:

Values—

Priorities—

Aims or goals—

2. The book of Ecclesiastes is even more skeptical about life's meaning and purpose than Psalm 90. But a recurring phrase in the book specifies the limited viewpoint to which its skepticism applies. What is that limited arena? (See the last phrase in Eccles. 1:3 and 2:11.)

32

Singing with the Spirit and the Understanding

"Sing praises to God, sing praises! Sing praises to our King, sing praises! For God is the King of all the earth; sing praises with understanding."—Psalm 47:6,7

There is no shortage of songs in the world, but not all of them praise God. In fact, many parents are understandably concerned about the corrupting influence of some music—and especially the sensual or violent lyrics bombarding youth from the arena of pop music.

Anna and I were very concerned about one such song that our son was required to sing at his grade school graduation exercises. It was a New Age rock piece and included words that were hardly edifying. After the ceremony I asked our son about it—not criticizing him at all, because I trusted him. I was simply probing to see to what degree he had been paying attention to the pagan lyrics the class had sung together. "How did you feel about singing that song?" I asked.

"Oh, that," this 12-year-old said. "I don't even know all the words, Dad. I just heard enough when we started practicin' it—ya' could tell it wasn't the kinda' song that we'd sing. Anyway, after that I stopped singin' the words, an' when everyone else sang I'd just sing in the Spirit!"

It was so terrific! He was just a boy, but he already knew the difference between "the song of the Lord" and the songs of the world, and knew the benefit of appropriating the "spiritual song." And best, the lyrics of the song mattered to him!

Music mattered to the psalmist, too, who admonished Israel to sing "with understanding." Later, the apostle Paul would echo this teaching: "I will sing with the spirit, and I will also sing with the understanding" (1 Cor. 14:15). Paul was especially concerned here that those in the congregation gifted with a song in a tongue granted by the Holy Spirit, also render them into a language that visitors could understand.

However, in our own assemblies today, how often, even in our own language, are songs merely mouthed—without vital understanding. In such instances, it hardly matters how holy or filled with the Spirit the song writer was. The composer's Spirit-fullness is no substitute for each would-be worshiper's "singing with the understanding."

Further, we all need discernment in the presentation

of Christian music. Perhaps you, as I, have been around the music of worship long enough to appreciate the need for Spirit-led and sensitively ministered worship in song. Periodically, some artists lose their bearings, and become more preoccupied with verifying their status as being "as good as secular musicians," and forget their primary ministry to the Lord. I am certainly not saying that we shouldn't cultivate our best talents and hone our skills to the sharpest as we offer our music to God. But I'm simply affirming the obvious: Holy Spirit enablement, joined to sensitivity in understanding, can cause a song to soar. With such balance it can flow to God's honor and glory better through a dedicated, single-minded heart, than through a technically-accurate but double-minded musician whose spirit is not in tune with *the* Spirit.

Someone once said to a leader at our church, "I don't know what Pastor Jack is doing, having us spend so much time singing. I guess *he* just likes it." The truth is, we do nothing in our gatherings just because I or anyone else "like it." We've targeted on larger purposes than private taste. The music the gathered church raises to God is crucial to what happens *among* us as well as *in* us. Our singing is not a preliminary "warm-up" to the "main event" called the sermon. It is an integral part of the worship, made vibrantly alive *in* us as we "sing with the Spirit and with the understanding also." It's to all our wisdom to learn such a way.

Praise in Prayer

We praise You, Lord, for the song You have put in our hearts, and for the musical gifts that enliven our assemblies. Grant that our minds and spirits will be in tune with Your eternal will. Through Jesus Christ our Lord, Amen.

Selected Readings

Psalm 30:11-12   Isaiah 12
Psalm 33:1-5   Acts 16:25-34

Praise in Practice

1. Obtain a hymnbook and examine the words of some of the old standby favorites to see if you understand all the lyrics. Look especially at "Night with Ebon Pinion" (What kind of night is that?), and "Come Thou Fount of Every Blessing" (What is an *Ebenezer?*).

2. Read Ephesians 5:17-21 and Colossians 3:16. What are the characteristics, purpose and result of singing, and the kinds of songs to be used in worship, according to these passages?

3. Enjoy a time of singing favorite "spiritual songs."

33
The Fellowship of Worship

> *"I proclaim righteousness in the great assembly; I do not seal my lips, as you know, O Lord. I do not hide your righteousness in my heart; I speak of your faithfulness and salvation. I do not conceal your love and your truth from the great assembly."*—Psalm 40:9,10 *(NIV)*

The joys of private praise are readily matched by the joys of corporate praise. Small wonder the Word enjoins that we "not forsake the assembling of ourselves together" (Heb. 10:25). In the Psalms, repeated references to sharing the things of God "in the great assembly" emphasize the same truth: Worship involves the whole people of God, not just individuals. God's righteousness and love and truth are too momentous to be hidden in the heart. The spirit of praise begs to "go public"!

Some folk have difficulty with the "structure" this

requires. Biblically, however, there is no way around it. In Scripture, worship extends beyond the spontaneous moments of private praise. It also involves a *time*, a *place* and a *people*.

Toward the end of his third missionary journey, the apostle Paul wanted to say farewell to his dear friends in the city of Troas, on the northwest coast of Asia Minor. Apparently he arrived there on what would have been a Sunday by our calendars, for he deliberately waited seven days in order to be with the brethren "on the first day of the week, when the disciples came together to break bread" (Acts 20:7).

Worship therefore involves a specific *time*. No less than in the Sabbath-worship of the Old Testament, believers today need this regular time of reprieve for our bodies and refreshment for our souls. If you are unable to keep this appointment with the Lord and your congregation on the first day of the week, it's important to work out another time when you can worship with them. We still need a "sabbath" on which our bodies can experience a reprieve, and our souls can be refreshed.

Worship involves a specific *place*. The Jews worshiped together first in the Tabernacle, then the Temple. Early Christians met together "from house to house" (Acts 2:46; 20:20). Resist the pretentious notions of the supposed purist who argues against church buildings. God likes them! While a place large enough to accommodate hundreds of worshipers can acknowledgeably become either the life or the death of a congregation, there is still nothing inherently wrong with such. The fellowship of worship *requires* a place in practical terms and *recommends* a place on biblical terms.

And worship involves a specific *people.* The New Testament knows nothing of highly individualistic believers who refuse to fellowship where some sort of functional leadership structure is present. From the very beginning of the story of salvation, when God called Abraham to follow Him, He has a special people, Israel, in mind. By faith, believers in Jesus become the new Israel (Gal. 6:16). And members of that worshiping community are urged to "submit" to each other (1 Cor. 16:15,16), and to "obey those who rule over you" (Heb. 13:17).

In submitting to water baptism we are not only identifying with submitting to Christ, we are also submitting to the Body and to the brothers and sisters in the Body: "For by one Spirit we were all baptized into one body" (1 Cor. 12:13). When we obediently respond to this call of the Spirit, we become united in a great fellowship designed by the Father, "to the intent that now the manifold wisdom of God might be made known by the church to the principalities and powers in the heavenly places" (Eph. 3:10). Thus the worshiping church as a submitted church becomes the victorious church!

Praise in Prayer

Thank You, O Lord, for the honor of being a limb—a living member—of the Body of Christ. Thank You also for the Body itself. Help me to be a smoothly functioning member in the fellowship of praise and worship; that hell's rebellion

be smashed by the Holy Spirit of submission
manifest in me and those with whom I worship.
Through Jesus Christ our Lord, Amen.

Selected Readings

Psalm 63:1-5   1 Corinthians 1:10-17

Acts 2:40-47   Philippians 2:1-4

Praise in Practice

1. Read Psalm 67, and count the number of plural references. Are there any singulars at all—any "me's" or "I's"?

2. Do you think Christians today emphasize the private or "singular" nature of the faith to the neglect of the corporate fellowship?

34
Glory Lost, Glory Regained

"When I consider Your heavens, the work of Your fingers, the moon and the stars, which You have ordained, what is man that You are mindful of him, and the son of man that You visit him? For You have made him a little lower than the angels, and You have crowned him with glory and honor."—Psalm 8:3-5

Earlier, we dwelt to some extent on what it means to ascribe "glory" (Hebrew *chabod)* to God. But here the psalmist also speaks of a glory with which humans may be endowed. Is it sheer arrogance to apply the same word to people that we use to describe God? No, but rather it is a humbling reminder that we were created in His glorious image, only "a little lower than the angels."

But merely to mention our exalted origins is also to recall that the glory of man was dimmed, shattered in the

Fall. Since Adam and Eve, the shame of sin has clouded the image of God in all of us. We should note that through sin what was lost was glory. More than the nakedness they discovered, the shame of our forebears was a lost dimension of sufficiency in God's adequacy. That loss was a glory that God intended for each individual to have, and one which He comes to restore in Christ.

As "glory" is *chabod* in Hebrew, so the "loss of glory" has a Hebrew name, pronounced *Ick-chabod.* It's simply "chabod" preceded by a negative, and means literally "In-glorious" or "Where is the glory?" Do you remember Ichabod Crane, the awkward character in Washington Irving's classic tale of "The Headless Horseman"? His ungainly appearance and less-than-noble bearing doubtless occasioned the author's choice of his name. That name, Ichabod, also appears in the Bible, in an even more inglorious situation. In 1 Samuel 4 just after Eli the priest died, having heard the news that the Philistines had defeated Israel and captured the Ark of the Covenant, his daughter-in-law also died, in childbirth. Just before she passes away, she insists that her surviving child be named Ichabod—saying, "The glory has departed from Israel!" (vs. 21). The concept of human loss of destiny and dignity has seemed to distill in that episode and in that graceless name.

Sadly, in certain respects, we are all named "Ichabod," in that as sinners the glorious image of God in us has been marred. Gladly, however, the story of salvation is the story of "Glory Regained" through Jesus and His perfect offering for sin. His coming to save us has fulfilled the prophetic promise that "the glory of the Lord shall be revealed, and all flesh shall see it together" (Isa. 40:5). Thus the gospel is the story of overcoming "Ichabod" with reinstated *chabod*—of conquering sin with grace and reinstating glory! Just as through sin, the Ark of the Covenant was lost, and thereby the symbol of God's presence removed from among His people, so through Christ, the glory has been returned. "Behold, the tabernacle of God is with men, and He will dwell with them, and they shall be His people, and God Himself will be with them and be their God" (Rev. 21:3). Glory to God for His triumphant work through Jesus our Lord!

Praise in Prayer

I praise You, Father, for creating persons in Your image. Help me to overcome the shame of having dimmed the brightness of Your glory. As I have trusted and obeyed Your glorious Son and received His life and light, now O Father grant a reinstatement of Your glory upon my life and through my life, for Your glory, Amen.

Selected Readings

Psalm 3	John 17:20-26
Psalm 16:5-11	Romans 5:12-21

Praise in Practice

1. Which is more vivid in your daily awareness, the picture of yourself as bearing the image of God, or as a

sinner who has dimmed that image? What practical difference in your self-image does your answer make?

2. In 1 Corinthians 15:41, Paul says, "There is one glory of the sun, another glory of the moon." If we compared the glory of persons and the glory of God to these heavenly bodies, which might stand for man's glory, and which for God's? Why?

3. In what practical ways can Christians glorify God without trying to glorify themselves beyond what Christ has done for them?

35

You Can't Escape Him—and Aren't You Glad!

"Where can I go from Your Spirit? Or where can I flee from Your presence? If I ascend into heaven, You are there; if I make my bed in hell, behold, You are there."—Psalm 139:7,8

This poignant psalm seems at first to picture a person in flight from God and His Spirit, fearing God as being something like a cosmic cop in pursuit of a spiritual fugitive. Of course the writer discovers that there is no escape. It would be foolish to expect to flee to heaven to hide from the Spirit, for that is His domain. Even hell cannot hide us from Him—the word here being *sheol*, which refers to the grave, not the place of everlasting punishment. The message is clear: God will find us, whether we are "flying high" or "lying low."

Then, from an apparent context of despair, a strongly positive aspect appears. The psalmist's tone turns to the glad confession that God's omnipresent Spirit is not pursuing him to do him harm, but to lead him and guide him (see vs. 10). It's a wonderful advance note on the New Testament's unfolding of the comforting presence of the Holy Spirit: the Paraclete promised to "abide with you forever" (John 14:16). Our praise deserves to be regularly punctuated with continual gratitude for His real presence and power.

Against the spirit of a materialistic, spiritually blinded age, in which so many neither perceive nor believe in anything that isn't physically perceptible or tangible, praise God with me for the Holy Spirit! The psalmist's refreshing reminder that the Spirit *is omnipresent* (i.e. *everywhere!*) is a precious truth. It announces to us: You will be besieged by *no* state of mind, pursued by *no* terror, and threatened by *no* imprisoning effect of hell that the Spirit cannot penetrate, conquer or overthrow!

Our humanness may at times feel embarrassed at this inescapable Presence, wishing we could hide our darker actions and thoughts. But in our wisest moments, or most desperate, we are rejoiced that He pursues us, especially in times when weakness or temptation ambushes us.

Let every believer praise God for the Holy Spirit's being *our Helper in prayer.* "For we do not know what we should pray for as we ought, but the Spirit Himself makes intercession for us with groanings which cannot be uttered...according to the will of God" (Rom. 8:26,27).

Let every believer praise God for the overwhelming

power of the Spirit. He is THE Force—the *real* one—not the cultish or ethereal "Force" of a Star Wars flick. He is the personally caring, mightily attentive-to-us, Holy Spirit of God! He "was hovering over the face of the waters" when the creation was spoken into existence (Gen. 1:2); He was the One who came upon Jesus at His baptism (Matt. 3:16); and He's the One who still baptizes believers today with empowering grace (see Luke 24:49 and Acts 2:4).

Let every believer praise God for the Spirit's *indwelling and leading* in our everyday lives, for the freedom His presence brings from oppressive "religious" rules, and for the rich fruit He begets—the love and joy, the peace and patience He produces in the life of the committed Christian (see Gal. 5:16-26).

In all these and a host of other ways, the Holy Spirit is our assurance; He makes real a higher and deeper realm than the mere material world about us. Yet He is so practical, and life "in the Spirit" so workable in a workaday world. He has not called us to some disembodied existence in order to make us "spiritual," but His power permeates our daily reality with the new wine of renewal; and He is fully available to each of us who *ask* for His presence (Luke 11:13).

Who would *ever* want to flee from *that* presence?!

Praise in Prayer

Holy Spirit, I praise You for surrounding me with Your abiding presence and dynamic availability. Help me to live in the power of Your

indwelling and fullness; and to walk in simple,
trusting dependence on Your promised guid-
ance. In Jesus' name, Amen.

Selected Readings

Psalm 139:1-18   Romans 8:26-30
John 16:5-15   Galatians 5:16-26

Praise in Practice

1. Why is it important to refer to the Holy Spirit as "He" (as in John 16:5-15), instead of "it"?

2. Share any evidence you have experienced of the reality of the Holy Spirit.

3. Do you think even Christians are tempted to think of reality in terms of the merely material?

36

Aggressiveness in Worship

"Let the saints be joyful in glory; let them sing aloud on their beds. Let the high praises of God be in their mouth, and a two-edged sword in their hand."—Psalm 149:5,6

In calling us to worship, God is up to far more than cultivating a band of humble worshipers; He is building an army of triumphant warriors. This is why our text speaks of "the high praises of God" in the same breath as "a two-edged sword." Of course we are dealing here not with weapons of carnal warfare, but with putting our words into action by boldly going on the offensive of faith—*acting* on the promises of the God we praise.

Turn again to that dramatic scene in 2 Chronicles 20. King Jehoshaphat, undermanned and relatively powerless, has been brought word that "a great multitude is coming against you" (vs. 2). Listen to it, fellow-servant!

You know, or know someone who knows, the empty feeling: word comes of a dread disease leaving only weeks or months to live; an accountant's report says the business is going under; a loved one tells you your relationship is about to be broken in divorce or abandonment. This text gives direction on what can be done in such moments, something besides resigning to a passive prayer for strength. There are four action steps—ways to "take up the sword" of worship.

First, the king proclaimed a *fast* (vs. 3). Is fasting foreign to your experience? Don't let it be. Fasting is an aggressive way to affirm the promised power of the spirit over the flesh. It is an explicit way to reinforce the priority of prayer and to seek God at extra times each day. When facing crucial battles such as the one which confronted Jehoshaphat, be ready to deny the flesh as a sign that your trust is not in human energy but in the power of the Spirit.

Next, the king and the people *prayed* (vs. 6). And while their prayer confessed that "we have no power" (vs. 12), it wasn't a "Poor me" prayer! Instead of whining it roared, ascribing to God power and authority over the enemy. Such a prayer of petition is admittedly prayed out of deep need, but it nonetheless boldly affirms God's power within His will.

Third, there was also a *remembrance of God's work* in history (vs. 7). With praise they remember the story of God's people—the Exodus from Egypt, God's care in the wilderness, the conquest of Canaan. "Remembering" is a mighty source of confidence that God is able and will again deliver and save. Reviewing testimonies or "remembering" at the Lord's Table are ways we can do this.

And fourth, there was a *prophetic utterance* (vss. 14-17). Be open to the Holy Spirit's prophetic word among us as a people. He's still assuring us: "The battle is not yours, but God's!" (vs. 15), and He will faithfully unfold God's will for us in our own immediate situations.

Uncommonly threatening situations call for uncommonly strong response; for taking up a "two-edged sword" in a spiritual sense—*aggressively* trusting God, *forcefully* throwing ourselves in worship at His feet, and *boldly* brandishing the spiritual weapons Jehoshaphat used. They still work, to put doubt and fear and anxiety to flight.

Praise is not passive. It can be our boldest stand against the threats of the enemy.

Praise in Prayer

O God my Strength, I praise You for coming to me in my weakness. Grant that I may not use my humanity as a cloak for cowardice, but teach me to boldly affirm Your power to give me Your victory over the enemy. In Jesus' name, Amen.

Selected Readings

2 Chronicles 20:22-29   Psalm 138
Psalm 84:8-12   Acts 4:13-31

Praise in Practice

1. Can you share an experience when God came to your aid when you were facing a crisis?

2. If you have ever fasted, describe your experience. Did it help you focus on the spirit over the flesh? What advice about fasting would you offer someone considering it?

3. How can you discern when God wants you to relax and let Him work in your life, and when He is calling for aggressive action on your part?

4. What do you think of the old saying that we should "Pray as though everything depended on God, and work as though everything depended on us"?

37

The Heavens Declare His Glory— Join Them!

"The heavens declare the glory of God; and the firmament shows His handiwork. Day unto day utters speech, and night unto night reveals knowledge."—Psalm 19:1,2

I wonder if God can place as much confidence in us as He has in creation? One of the beauties of the Psalms is their affirmation that the physical realm gives eloquent testimony to the glory of God, that creation testifies to the grandeur of the Creator. Humans could take lessons!

Here we read how the beauty of the skies bear witness to God's glory. "The heavens" and "the firmament" are not two different things but are an example of Hebrew "parallelism"—saying the same thing in different but parallel ways. By these terms the psalmist draws evidence of God's majestic glory from the beauty of a sunset, from the unending variation of cloud formations and from the "tabernacle" or "tent" in which the sun runs its daily circuit from east to west (vss. 5,6).

Toward the end of the book of Job, he dwells on the same theme. When God confronts Job with his own pitifully finite wisdom, paling before such "natural" creation wonders as: how the earth "sits" on its invisible foundations, how the boundaries of the seas are set, how the expanse of the earth is spread—the nature of light, sun and stars, the entire ecological system, the awesome power of violent weather and the wondrous ways of animal life—all are marshalled in splendor as witness to God's greatness (see chs. 38-40).

These wonders call us to profound appreciation for the created order, a praising both in humility before God's glory and with a sense of responsibility for our role as stewards of this splendor. Such praise ought to remind us of our assignment as humans to care for creation, too, as the Bible account affirms. (See Gen. 1:26-31.)

It is in the glory light of all this evidence of God's person and power in creation that the apostle Paul charged unbelief as inexcusable, and ingratitude as perverse; because God's invisible nature and attributes "are clearly seen, being understood by the things that are made" (Rom. 1:18-21). Why, then, do some refuse to believe? Sometimes, surely, through thoughtlessness, while at other times because the awesome truths about God imbedded in creation have been stubbornly "suppressed" (vs. 18). There is often an immoral dimension to unbelief, a persistence in corrupt lusts that denies God's authority and glory: Some "did not like to retain God in their knowledge," so God "gave them up" (vv. 24-30).

But in contrast, to those of us who will open to the wonders of creation, every element of it speaks of His majesty and power. Hear Psalm 148 burst forth: "Praise Him, sun and moon; praise Him, all you stars of light! Praise Him, you heavens of heavens, and you waters above the heavens!...Sea creatures...fire and hail, snow and clouds; stormy wind,...mountains and all hills; fruitful trees and all cedars; beasts and all cattle; creeping things and flying fowl;...Let them praise the name of the Lord!" (Ps. 148:3-13).

Let us all join in!

Praise in Prayer

When I behold Your heavens and the other works of Your hands, I can only stand in awe and amazement, O Lord. Help me to view whatever man can learn about Your world as further evidence of Your majesty and power. And may multitudes be turned to You as mankind beholds Your creation handiwork, Amen.

Selected Readings

Psalm 33:6-9   Jeremiah 31:35-37
Psalm 89:5-13   Romans 1:18-25

Praise in Practice

1. Describe an experience that enabled (or enables) you to see the handiwork of God in creation.

2. What was the reaction of Job when confronted with the majesty of God as manifest in His creation? (See Job 42:1-6.)

3. Do you think modern science generally manifests this kind of humility at the wonders of the "natural world"? Does godly awe at the secrets of nature mean that science should not probe them and try to understand them?

38

Shout It Out!

---

*"Oh, clap your hands, all you peoples! Shout to
God with the voice of triumph! For the Lord
Most High is awesome; He is a great King over
all the earth."*—Psalm 47:1,2

Don't pick up the Psalms if you want your worship
devotion to keep cool and sedate. The psalmist frequently casts restraint and so-called social correctness to
the winds. His heart explodes; he's too full to cap the
artesian flow of the joy in the Lord he feels!

There is a holy wisdom in shouting even though it
sometimes meets with resistance among "proper" Christians who have been shaped by today's social sophisti-
cations. For David, it was an outburst born of godly
wisdom. For us, it may seem that it borders on the
fanatic. I confess to feeling this way at times. But I'm
also bewildered at times by the much-too-willingness
of some dear souls who seem ready to shout at the
drop of a hat (or even if a hat doesn't drop!). Pride can
easily concoct reasons for avoiding joyous responsive-

ness, even when a shout would be *very* appropriate. I may argue for "the dignity of silence" if I choose, or even exploit the Bible's admonition to do things "decently and in order" (1 Cor. 14:40), to proof-text my prideful reserve.

However, the psalmist seems to have a broader standard of "decent" expressiveness than some of us "modern" worshipers. Let me share a personal experience that illustrates the importance of conforming our worship more by God's Word than by modern standards.

It was at a Sunday morning service some years ago, and for no apparent reason a depressing heaviness hung over the congregation. It was more than a human reaction to an overcast sky, or the general weariness brought on by a busy season; far more than the social fatigue people bear due to a tough time being navigated by the community. "This is a spirit of oppression," the Holy Spirit whispered to me. "Call the people to resist it with a shout. Magnify the victory of the Cross, and that spirit will be overthrown."

I knew I faced a crossroads. How could I lead the people to respond to the dictates of the Spirit, and not to think they were being manipulated into a foolish exercise by a "loose-cannon" leader? I took a deep breath, paused, and gently said: "Church, I need to stop here in this service for a few minutes. I need to talk with you about something very important, about something I believe we need to do—something that will only have spiritual power if we all *together* understand and apply its meaning."

They were fully attentive, recognizing a "special

moment" by my tone. I proceeded to identify the spirit of heaviness and oppression, and I explained the biblical basis for dealing boldly with such brazen attacks from Satan. I recalled the shout at Jericho, Jesus' shout "It is finished!" at the Cross, and the shout prophesied when He comes again. On those grounds, I urged that we resist that heaviness with "the voice of triumph." And then...we shouted! My, how we did shout! To the accompaniment of the organ's loud fanfare, we put Jesus' name on our lips and magnified the victory of the Cross to break the powers of hell.

And those powers were broken—right there. The atmosphere changed—we sang "All Hail the Power of Jesus' Name"—and a new spirit of responsiveness and openness pervaded the assembly. I might add as well, many came to know Jesus Christ as Savior—amid shouts of praise!

And as for the spirit of heaviness and oppression? In the power of the Spirit and to the glory of Jesus' name, we simply "shouted it out!"

Praise in Prayer

Lord, we know Your glory is worth shouting about! But some of us have backgrounds and inhibitions that make it difficult to express the exaltation we feel. Grant that mere human restraints will not repress bold declarations of praise You have summoned in your Word; and grant that we will be guided more by what You find appropriate than by the world-minded sense of "propriety" which would silence the shout of triumph. Through Christ we pray, Amen.

Selected Readings

Joshua 6:1-5,20   Psalm 35:22-28
Psalm 32   Isaiah 44:21-23

Praise in Practice

1. Think about and discuss openly any reservations you may have about the shout of joy in worship. Are any of your reservations the result of pride or fear?

2. What enables people who would never shout in worship to get hoarse from shouting at a sports contest? Are any of the reasons shouting seems appropriate at such events applicable to times of praise and worship?

3. What effect or role did shouting have in the battle of Jericho? (See Joshua 6.)

39

Singing the Song of God in a Strange Land

"By the rivers of Babylon, there we sat down, yea, we wept when we remembered Zion. We hung our harps upon the willows in the midst of it. For....how shall we sing the Lord's song in a foreign land?"—Psalm 137:1,2,4

In my book, *Taking Hold of Tomorrow,* I relate how during my childhood, when I was five years old, my family's move from Southern California caused me to leave all my friends. We settled in Montana and I entered first grade, adjusting fairly quickly even though being the "new kid on the block" is never easy. Then, about the time I was feeling that Montana was home, we moved again—this time to Oakland, California—and I had to go through the adjustment process again.

Life stabilized, and by the time I made it to the fifth grade, among my "credits" was membership in the traffic patrol—jaunty hats and sweater stripes and all! But wait! Now on the brink of sixth grade and student office, we moved across town, and there went my friends and status. Later, after becoming a pretty fair basketball player, an injured knee broke my hope of high school stardom.

How often life's "moves" and "changes" put us in a "strange land." But hear the psalmist, for he also understands: How difficult to sing the Lord's song in a strange land, when things become "foreign" to our plans. This psalm probably refers to the season of exile the kingdom of Judah experienced when many were led captive to Babylon due to the nation's disobedience. No doubt you may well identify with them, for there are enough moves, upset situations and broken families in our own world for many of us to feel muted—not really ready to sing—silenced in new surroundings.

You will recall with me how God's faithfulness enabled many exiles to return later on. They rebuilt the Temple, restored their family homes and worshiped again in the place they had longed to see recovered. Still, it is apparent that many of those who remained in Babylon did learn to sing the Lord's song there after all, confirmed by archaeologists who today have found evidence of a thriving Jewish community there from about this period. The message is moving, for we see songs which brought *re*-covery and songs which made *dis*-covery; a lesson that we can raise our psalms of praise to the Lord wherever we are—not just geographically but emotionally as well.

Disappointing transitions and setbacks and strange settings can spin our plans around, and set our life askew. Life doesn't always work out the way it appeared it might. But our real challenge is to not let circumstances set boundaries that seem to block our prayers and thwart our attempts to continue in the song and spirit of praise. Worship frees us from such boundaries!

You don't have to pretend. We don't have to be stoic about our feelings. Be honest and admit that it's just easier to praise in some settings than in others. But then, go ahead and praise the Lord anyway! We honor Him the God who transcends the boundaries of nations, the walls of familiar churches, the barriers of mere states of mind and the situations that disappoint us. Sing! However "strange" or foreign your situation. You'll find His presence making the strangest "place" in your life into a "hometown" with Him close at hand.

Praise in Prayer

O God everywhere present, I praise You for being available regardless of time and place and circumstance. Help me to be at home in Your world, wherever I am, so I may be faithful in praise in season and out of season, full or in need, near or far. Through Christ our Lord, Amen.

Selected Readings

Praise in Practice

1. Have you ever made a move, lived in a foreign country, or had any other disruption in your life that made it difficult for you to focus on praise and worship?

2. Have you ever become so attached to a church building or a particular style of church architecture that changing it created a problem?

3. How did living as captives in Babylon affect the worship of the "three Hebrew children" in Daniel 3:8-18?

4. What indication had God given Daniel and his three friends that He would be with them in Babylon as they were faithful to Him? (See Dan. 1:5-21.)

40

Where the Glory Dwells

---

*"O God, You are my God; early will I seek You;
my soul thirsts for You; my flesh longs for You
in a dry and thirsty land where there is no
water. So I have looked for You in the sanctuary, to see Your power and Your glory."*
—Psalm 63:1,2

It's easy to understand David's thirst, both for water and
for God, while he was fleeing for his life from Saul in
the arid wilderness above the Dead Sea. What is harder
to understand is the tendency of some believers today
who seem unable to accept spiritual nourishment anywhere except at the newest and most sensational spiritual "show" in town at the moment; people who presume that more of God's glory is "over there"—
somewhere—anywhere but where he or she is at the
moment.

The place where God's glory dwells has an interesting history that should make us cautious about church-hopping. In the days when the Israelites left Egypt, God made His presence known in the pillars of cloud and fire. Then, in giving of the Law through Moses, He instructed His people to build the Ark of the Covenant—a portable chest about four feet long, two feet wide and two feet tall. This "Ark," containing the Ten Commandments, was the center point of their worship; the place where God's presence was made known to the people during their wandering through the wilderness. God had promised, "And there I will meet with you" (Exod. 25:22). And He did.

Within the Tabernacle, the great "tent of meeting," the Ark was positioned in the innermost area—the most sacred room, called the holy of holies. It was there the Ark remained when the Tabernacle was at rest.

Later, the same Ark was placed in the magnificent Temple King Solomon built, as God graciously showed His readiness and pleasure to transfer His appointed meeting place to that more permanent earthly abode.

But it did not remain that way. Through unfaithfulness, God's people living in such blatant disobedience to Him that He allowed the Temple to be destroyed, the Ark finally disappeared from the pages of history. His ancient people were carried away captive to other lands, so *now,* where could His presence be experienced?

Let the New Testament answer the question: The "glory" attending the Ark is now promised to us, "Now to Him who is able to do exceedingly abundantly above all that we ask or think, according to the power that works in us, to Him be glory IN THE CHURCH by Christ Jesus throughout all ages, world without end" (Eph. 3:20,21, emphasis mine). *The people of God now house the glory of God. The Ark has been transferred to us!*

This means that the holy objects in the Ark are now to be found, in a spiritual sense, in *the worshiper*—not at some point of spiritual fascination to which the superficial seeker races. God has come to dwell with and in *you*—in me—in us! Just as the Ark contained the tables on which the Law was given to Moses, He now writes His Word on our hearts. Just as the Ark held a container of manna, so God's Spirit has been given to daily assist us with miracle grace. And just as the Ark contained Aaron's rod that budded, we have been invested with eternal life and a grand capacity for continued growth. (I'll resist the temptation to say that God can make a "bloomin' somethin'" out of you!)

The point is clear: The glory of God now dwells in *you*. To restlessly seek it in outside pursuits or outside your fellowship might say more about our own unreceptivity to God's glory than about our congregation's. Yes! We should all certainly find a faithful congregation, one where the Word is proclaimed with balance and grace, and where the Spirit of God is made welcome. But dear ones, let us affirm that under those conditions the Ark of God comes to rest, and the glory of God finds a home—and let us rest, too, with prepared hearts for His indwelling.

Praise in Prayer

I long to be in Your Presence and experience Your glory, O God. Help me to nourish Your indwelling in my own heart as my first responsibility, and to do what I can to lovingly contribute to my congregation's gatherings, making them times when You rejoice to be present among us. In Jesus' strong name I pray, Amen.

Selected Readings

Exodus 25:10-22   1 Corinthians 3:1-17
1 Kings 9:1-9   1 Corinthians 6:12-20

Praise in Practice

1. Describe any experience you may have had when you felt beyond question that you were in the presence of God. Do you think it was the result of physical appointments, such as a sanctuary? Of faithful preaching of the Word? Of inspirational music? Or were you alone, perhaps in a place apart?

2. What specific qualities do you look for in a place to assemble regularly with brothers and sisters in Christ? With the help of a concordance, see if you can supply a Bible basis for each quality.

41
The Christ of the Psalms

"I will declare the decree: the Lord has said to Me, 'You are My Son, today I have begotten You. Ask of Me, and I will give You the nations for Your inheritance, and the ends of the earth for Your possession.'"—Psalm 2:7,8

One of the unique features of the Psalms is David's praise of One greater—One to come. Over and over devout Jews would ask of this passage and others like it, "Of whom does the prophet speak?" While David, as we are, was God's son in the created sense, the Holy Spirit gave him words about another Son in an "only begotten" sense beyond what David may have understood. The world would have to wait until Jesus came—until the coming of the Messiah—to hear it explained that "my Lord" and "my Son" are actually and ultimately Jesus Christ Himself (see Heb. 1:5).

This unique feature of the Psalms makes them an appropriate vehicle for us to praise the uniqueness of Christ. So pause with me. Let's just spend time focusing on how there is none other like Jesus. The following is excerpted from a sermon on His uniqueness which I brought to nearly 3,000 leaders in England recently.

Jesus is the one and only Second Adam, sent to salvage and restore what the First Adam lost.

He is the unique Virgin-born Son of God, sinless Man; the Incarnate Truth, the manifest fullness of the Father.

He is the only substitutionary Lamb of God—dying according to the Scriptures; given to redeem from sin all who believe.

Jesus is the Crucified One who was buried and who rose again—literally, physically and in power—on the third day, according to the Scriptures.

He is the One and only One who, upon completely providing the grounds of all human redemption, has ascended to heaven to take His seat at the right hand of the Father.

He is the One who has poured out the Holy Spirit to all those who obey Him.

He is the One who ever lives to make intercession for us.

He is the One who will soon descend and be revealed as King of kings and Lord of lords, to receive His redeemed Church to be with Him forever.

His alone is the blood that can redeem;

His alone the body broken for our healing;

His alone is the sacrifice that can satisfy the price of atonement for sin;

His alone the death that can purchase life for sinful man.

His alone is the righteousness that can justify us before God, establishing us as "not guilty" in His court;

His alone the power that can break the chains of death—for it was not possible that He could be held by it; and

He alone, in rising, has verified to us the promise of eternal life.

Soldiers sent to capture Him returned saying, "We've never heard any man speak like this man."

Disciples witnessing His stilling the storm said, "What manner of man is this, that even the wind and the sea obey Him?"

The Roman centurion watching Him die declared, "Surely this man was the Son of God."

Thomas, at first doubting, was led finally to confess that in the resurrected Jesus he saw, "My Lord and my God!"

God? Yes, for this is the One and only One who is enthroned far above all principalities and power and might and dominion, and every name that is named, not only in this age but in the world to come, world without end, Amen.

Praise in Prayer

I exalt You, Lord Jesus, as the unique Son, as King of kings and Lord of lords. I confess that there is no other name in heaven or on earth by which we can be saved. Help my life to reflect my acknowledgment of You as my personal King, Amen.

Selected Readings

Genesis 15:1-6   Acts 4:5-12
Isaiah 7:10-14; 9:2-7   Hebrews 1

Praise in Practice

1. Although this chapter emphasizes the uniqueness of Christ and the Christian faith, in what ways are we indebted to the Jews, the family of Abraham, for our faith?

2. What implications does Christ's uniqueness have as far as our priorities and loyalties are concerned? For evangelism?

42

Let the King of Glory In!

---

*"Lift up your heads, O you gates! And lift them
up, you everlasting doors! And the King of
glory shall come in. Who is this King of glory?
The Lord of hosts, He is the King of glory."*
—Psalm 24:9,10

Throughout the Psalms there is an interplay between
David, king of Israel, and, in a prophetic sense, Christ—
the King from whom David received his own throne. In
Psalm 24 the rich imagery is of a great king approaching
a city under his control. As he and his colorful
entourage approach the city gates, their presence is so
commanding that the gates—the city leaders who gathered there in counsel—are exhorted to attend to their
entry. The city and its inhabitants are to make the royal
party welcome. In writing, David proposes a royal welcome for the King of heaven.

Are the gates to our hearts prepared to give such

honor to the entry and enthronement of Christ, our King of glory? The question needs to be asked not because kingship is so unusual in our own days, but because it is so common! That is, *sovereignty*—the claim to rule—is almost as widespread as each of us free-willed human beings. Yet, though sovereignty abounds, the King of glory will tolerate no competition.

Not only do states, nations, kingdoms and governments claim sovereignty over individuals; individuals themselves claim it for themselves. No cry has been louder in our day than the demand for self-determination. And indeed such freedom is a God-endowed privilege invested in all persons by virtue of their having been created in the image of God.

But the *misapplication* of sovereignty is widespread, too. And this makes it all the more important that we identify the uniqueness of Christ's sovereignty. "Taking control of my own life," as we often hear, must be affirmed only under the superior rule of the King of glory.

Christ is King by virtue of His being *the Source of creation*. John's Gospel begins by recalling Genesis 1, when God spoke the universe into existence, and names Jesus as the creative Word behind it all (John 1:1-3,14). And in the Revelation, royal worshipers cast their own crowns aside, saying, "You are worthy, O Lord, to receive glory and honor and power; for You created all things" (Rev. 4:11).

Christ is King because He is *God's only begotten Son*. His royal status was recognized by other royalty at His birth, as the wise men from the East inquired, "Where is

He who has been born King of the Jews?" (Matt. 2:2). And toward the end of His earthly life, His kingship was pictured in the Triumphal Entry into the city of Jerusalem, in fulfillment of the prophecy, "Behold, your King is coming to you, lowly, and sitting on a donkey, a colt, the foal of a donkey" (Matt. 21:5).

That Christ is King was *announced by Peter at Pentecost* as he proclaims Jesus raised from the dead and exalted to the right hand of the throne of God! (Acts 2:32-36).

And Christ the King will come again from that throne in royal power. Thus it is *before Him* that all mankind will finally appear for review and judgment. Thus it is *by Him* that every person will be measured and either approved or disapproved. And thus it is *unto Him* that every being shall ultimately bow the knee, and that every tongue shall confess that Jesus Christ is Lord, to the glory of the Father.

Let every ear hear it! Let every heart-gate open freely for His entry, confessing with mind and heart and body, "You are the Christ, the Son of the Living God. You alone are King of kings, and Lord of hosts!"

Praise in Prayer

I praise You, King of heaven, for exercising Your power with such love and justice. I adore You, Lord over all the earth, for the blessings You distribute so freely to Your subjects. I honor You, King Jesus, as Master of my life, in Your own name, Amen.

Selected Readings

Psalm 29:8-11   Zechariah 9:9-17
Psalm 47   Revelation 14:14-16

Praise in Practice

1. Thinking of Christ as King, what terms would you use to describe His followers?

2. What implication for the self-image of the Christian can be drawn from the fact that Christ is King? (See Rev. 1:6.)

3. What part of our lives do we (do *you!*) have most difficulty subjecting to the Kingship of Jesus?

43

Gentle King: The Lion with a Shepherd's Heart

"The Lord is my shepherd; I shall not want. He makes me to lie down in green pastures; He leads me beside the still waters. He restores my soul...I will fear no evil."—Psalm 23:1-4

The preceding reflections focused on the kingship and might of our Lord Jesus Christ. Come now to the passage that is favorite to so many—perhaps, because in showing our Great King's might, His tender and compassionate heart is also revealed.

Oh, that we could incorporate this delicately balanced trait in our presentation of our King Jesus to all who don't know Him. Oh, that the spirit of judgmentalism might be broken by us who know the gentle leadership of the Shepherd, and who speak both—*the truth* and the *love* He manifests.

This is not to deny the frightening fate looming before those who turn their back on the message of salvation. But well may we try to recover the example of Jesus, who gave a King's clear *call* in an amazingly winsome *spirit*. Look at the evidence in John's Gospel; a clear fulfillment in Christ's earthly ministry of those traits David described of the Great Shepherd a thousand years before. He's a powerful yet gentle King; a Lion, with a Shepherd's heart for Lambs. For example:

- Jesus disavows judgmentalism as His mission, saying to His critics, "I judge no one. And yet if I do judge, My judgment is true" (John 8:15,16).
- Jesus avows forgiveness and divine justice as His task, telling a broken soul, "Neither do I condemn you; go and sin no more" (John 8:11).
- Jesus expresses the price of eternal gain and eternal loss without preachiness, declaring that God so loved the world that He gave His only Son to save the world, not to condemn it.

Here is the blend of truth and tenderness we seek as we proclaim the Kingship of Christ. We are commissioned to confront, but not contentiously. We are called to proclaim a Person, not to argue with people. Jesus asks us to declare His Person in the loving power of the Holy Spirit, not to dissect other religious systems in the pseudo-power of our own debating skills. We are not commissioned to condemn, but to be ambassadors with the hope-filled message, "Be reconciled to God!"

When we speak the truth in love, we can rely on the

Holy Spirit to penetrate hearts, unveil needs, convince people of the adequacy of the Lord Jesus Christ and draw people to Him. Ultimately, "It is the Spirit who bears witness, because the Spirit is truth" (1 John 5:6).

We are dealing here with emphasis, not with content. Because the heresy of universalism is always afoot, we do need to include the price of disobedience in our proclamation. "Knowing, therefore, the terror of the Lord, we persuade men" (2 Cor. 5:11). But this very fact must move us to be all the more gentle. The tone of our message is implied by these italicized words: "We are ambassadors for Christ, as though God were *pleading* through us: we *implore* you on Christ's behalf, be reconciled to God" (v. 20).

John's Gospel supremely exhibits the balance of *clear proclamation* with *a shepherd's spirit*. In it the brightness of Jesus' uniqueness is lifted up to draw people. Jesus is proclaimed as a unique Creator (John 1), and a miracle worker interested in the joy of people at a wedding, not just performing magical tricks (John 2). He offers people the compassionate option of being born again (John 3). He offers the thirsty Living Water (chap. 4) and the hungry the Bread of Life (chap. 6). He encourages the paralyzed to "Get up!" (chap. 5), then portrays Himself as the ultimate "getter-up"! "I am the Resurrection and the Life" (chap. 11). And He speaks tenderly of the coming Comforter (chaps. 14,16), about whom we shall have more to say in the next devotion.

With a world drowning in sin, our first task is to throw it a lifeline—not hold its head under and say, "See there!" The spirit of the Shepherd bids us find ways to gather His lost sheep, not ways to frighten them. And as we worship Him with these perspectives, that spirit will fill and overflow us for such outreach.

Praise in Prayer

Lord Jesus, thank You for being my tender Shepherd. Help me never to trade on or presume upon Your compassion and grace. But also help my words and my living be a warm, winsome witness of Your love and majesty. I ask in Your name, Amen.

Selected Readings

Psalm 23   Psalm 130
Psalm 78:34-39   Ephesians 1:3-14

Praise in Practice

1. Was your decision to follow Christ influenced more by the promise of salvation or the threat of condemnation?

2. Do you think that, logically, to mention *salvation* implies its opposite, *judgment*? If so, how can Christian proclamation emphasize salvation, as Jesus did?

44

Wanted: Hearts Where the Comforter Can Abide

"Reproach has broken my heart, and I am full of heaviness; I looked for someone to take pity, but there was none; and for comforters, but I found none."—Psalm 69:20

Once more, David's plight becomes an avenue of praise. In his flight from the jealous rages of Saul, David had sought comfort and refuge with Ahimelech, priest of Nob (1 Sam. 21), with Achish, king of Gath (chap. 21)—even with Israel's arch enemies, the Philistines (chap. 27). Yet he had found no comforter like the Lord; and he can finally say, "Let heaven and earth praise Him....For God will save Zion" (Ps. 69:34,35).

Under the New Covenant, the role of Comforter (Paraclete) is the Holy Spirit's specialty. Five times in

John's Gospel, Jesus promised specific benefits from this "Paraclete"—literally, one "called alongside" to act both as a comforter and an advocate. First, knowing that He would shortly be returning to the Father, Jesus promised that the Spirit-Comforter, or Helper, would *abide* with us forever (John 14:16). Praise God for the continuing presence of the indwelling, overflowing work of the Holy Spirit, given to us as a down payment or deposit as a pledge of the glory to come when Jesus returns (see 2 Cor. 1:22).

Second, Jesus promised that the Comforter would *teach* His disciples, bringing to their remembrance His words, and guiding them into all truth (John 14:26; 16:13). We can hardly imagine how bereft the disciples of Jesus would have been, and how impoverished we would be, had not the divine Helper inspired them to recall and record the teaching of Jesus in what has become the Scriptures of the New Testament. Further, though of less authority than the absolute finality of the written Word, the Church still continues to receive truth ignited through the Spirit's gift of prophecy. These "words" are greatly enabling, helping us to respond to new situations in the power and wisdom of the Spirit's prompting and edification (see Rom. 12:6; 1 Cor. 12:10; Eph. 4:11).

Third, the Comforter would also *testify* of Jesus (John 15:26). He does this by animating our witness and by confirming the Word of the gospel with signs of power and grace. The Holy Spirit has unlimited power to demonstrate through the Church that "Jesus is still alive and well," and that His Kingdom power is unrestricted by either flesh or devil.

Fourth, Jesus promised that the Helper would *convict* the world "of sin,...of righteousness,...of judgment" (John 16:9-11). Here is the Spirit's role to which I referred in our preceding devotion; the Holy Spirit working to convince and convict hearts that Jesus is Lord and Savior—a task impossible for mere humans, since only He sees into human hearts, and only He can touch them unto a full awareness of their need.

And finally, John records Jesus' promise that the Comforter would *glorify* Him. After Jesus' departure to the Father, the Holy Spirit forged His divine qualities into protective armor and sanctified character and clothed His followers with them to equip them to continue His ministry (see John 16:14,15).

What thrilling promises! Yet there is a condition. The construction of the original language in these five promises from John's Gospel indicates that *each of the last four ministries of the Comforter depends on our receptivity to the first.* That is, our benefiting from the Comforter's work in teaching of, testifying to, convincing of and glorifying Jesus *among* us, depends completely upon our openness to His *abiding* or *dwelling in* us.

There is a sobering and practical point to all this. The growth of both—the church and our own lives—as well as the impact of spiritual renewal on our souls, however grand it may have been, has no guaranteed future on its own momentum. Resting on past successes will not qualify us to claim the next millennium for God. Only by praying for fresh anointings of the Spirit to sensitize us to fresh opportunities and responsibilities can we realize the benefits of the Comforter in the days ahead.

Praise in Prayer

We praise You, Holy Father, for the gift of, and the gifts of, Your Holy Spirit. Oh, Spirit of God, grant that I may be receptive to Your steadfast, abiding work in me, so I may be a part of Your continuing ministry in my day, my home, my church family and in my world, Amen.

Selected Readings

Acts 8:15-17   1 Corinthians 12:1-11
Romans 8:26-30   Galatians 5:16-26

Praise in Practice

1. Take several moments to respond to Luke 11:13— in prayer, simply ask the Lord for a fuller measure of His Holy Spirit.

2. What life changes characterize those who are filled with the Spirit (see Galatians 5:16-26).

Note

Devotions 41-44 are adapted from the booklet "The Uniqueness of Christ" © 1991, Jack W. Hayford, page 15. Published by LIVING WAY MINISTRIES, Van Nuys, California.

45

Keys to Sustaining Faith (I)

"Save me, O God! For the waters have come up to my neck. I sink in deep mire, where there is no standing;...I am weary with my crying; my throat is dry; my eyes fail while I wait for my God."—Psalm 69:1-3

There is no weariness like the soul-weariness of which the psalmist speaks here. Quick surges of faith may occur in an inspirational moment, but how do you *sustain* faith during prolonged sickness, continued temptation or seemingly unending relational struggles? Here are three keys.

Feed on living bread. Jesus said, "Man shall not live by bread alone, but by every word that proceeds from the mouth of God" (Matt. 4:4). When you come to the end of yet another day that has drained your physical, emotional and spiritual strength, sit down and read the

Word of God. If you can't stay awake, stand up and read it aloud.

"But Jack, that's the very time I don't *feel* like reading the Bible. And besides, I never remember what I read." Dear one, you're not training for a Bible quiz—you're *eating*. I don't remember what I ate last Thursday, but it did my body good. I may not always remember brilliant flashes of insight which light up the dark recesses of my spirit, but my spirit is being fed by the Holy Spirit—who is both the Ever-present Comforter, and the Source of the Word of God (see John 16:13).

Stand above condemnation. The Adversary would like nothing better than to keep an already burdened spirit stooped even lower with a load of condemnation. This is that depression that comes when you can't help dwelling on all the reasons you don't deserve anything good in life. The accusing whispers seem to scream: "With my past, why should God answer my prayers?" "Guilt and heaviness, problems, are just what I deserve."

Condemnation can be relentless when we are in a certain frame of mind. We wake up to a cloudy morning and somehow we think it's our fault. We can't seem to wrench our mind away from "digging up bones"— uncovering past sins and shortcomings and failures, and sitting in the dirt staring at them.

Memorize 1 John 3:20,21 for such times: "If our heart condemns us, God is greater than our heart...if our heart does not condemn us, we have confidence toward God." John is dealing with the tension between conviction and condemnation. Conviction will draw you to Jesus; condemnation will make you tell yourself how little you deserve to be there. And of course we *don't* deserve His grace! But the next time lying condemnation whispers, "You don't deserve God's goodness," just reply: "Right! So now I'll just praise the Lord *again!!*"

And *give forgiveness freely.* There's nothing so wearying to the spirit as carrying around bitterness or rancor toward others. How easy it is to forget Matthew 6:12: "Forgive us our debts, *as we forgive our debtors.*" This means that if I insist on carrying a grudge against others, I can't even expect Jesus to lift the sense of my own burden from my soul! I consign myself to a double load.

The psalmist's determination to "wait for my God" may indicate admirable patience. But here is something you can do while you wait: Consciously and specifically forgive others. In developing the largeness of heart it takes to forgive others, your heart muscles will be strengthened to better cope with your own situation.

Praise in Prayer

I praise You, God of strength, for the power of Your Word, for Your indwelling Spirit, and for the gift of forgiveness. In times that call for sustained faith, help me to draw strength from the constancy of Your gifts. Through Christ our Lord, Amen.

Selected Readings

Psalm 69:13-18   Matthew 11:28-30
Psalm 119:25-32   Luke 6:35-38

Praise in Practice

1. What do you habitually do just before retiring at night? Read the paper? Work a crossword? Watch a late-night television program? Try reading a Bible passage or a devotional reading the last thing each night for a week. Report on any differences this makes in your outlook the next morning.

2. Meditate on whether you are harboring hard feelings toward anyone. Focus on the fact that God has forgiven you; then release any hard feelings toward another.

46

Keys to Sustaining Faith (II)

> *"Depart from me, all you workers of iniquity;
> for the Lord has heard the voice of my weep-
> ing. The Lord has heard my supplication; the
> Lord will receive my prayer."*—Psalm 6:8,9

It is often remarked that the "imprecatory psalms"—
those that call down judgment on the psalmist's enemies—have little application to *Christians*, since we are
taught to forgive our enemies. Since they were written
hundreds of years before Christ, it's hard to see how
these Psalms reveal the pattern of forgiveness established through Christ's cross. Yet these railings against
"workers of iniquity" are honest. And if I read "my
Adversary" when I come to "my enemies," I will see the
evil one these Psalms mean to address. I can also
release some healthy anger at Satan through declaring
these passages! What enabled the psalmist here to sur-

vive his enemies' onslaught until his prayers were answered? Join these three more "keys to sustaining faith" with those in our last study.

Offer praise amid turmoil. Let's deal with that oft-quoted passage, "In everything give thanks; for this is the will of God in Christ Jesus for you" (1 Thess. 5:18). Let's not make the mistake of thinking the Bible means "praise the Lord in the middle of catastrophes *because that is God's will for you.*" Many of your problems may well be Satan's work, not God's. But that verse does express divine wisdom. Praising God in the midst of difficulty stakes out God's territory over against Satan's. I'm sure it wasn't easy for the three Hebrew children in the book of Daniel to praise God in the midst of the fiery furnace. They were not praising the fire, but the presence of God with them *in* the fire. In times of difficulty, assert Jesus' overpowering presence by faith.

Sing about hope. Isaiah 54:1-3 tells us to sing when there is no life in the womb, and life will come forth. Not everyone has a biological womb, but everyone has a womb-shaped heart created for gestating dreams and carrying embryonic hopes. God says to *sing* over these, and He will bring new life from them. The song of faith builds bridges over nothingness, and God's power touches dreams and brings them to reality!

Is your faith-threatening darkness blacker than the jail in the city of Philippi in which Paul and Silas were confined? What could they do, there in the murky gloom? Why, they could sing! And God took the reverberations from their song of faith and magnified them into an earthquake that jarred open the jail doors. Don't forget the power of song to fulfill God's promise.

Finally, to sustain faith, let your problems find you *"continuing steadfastly in prayer"* (Rom. 12:12). Certainly we need regular occasions of prayer such as daily devotionals; but Paul has in mind here a constant *attitude* of prayer that we must develop in order to sustain faith in difficult times. This is the prayer breathed while we wait for the traffic signal to change; the inner hope expressed as you sit down at your desk first thing in the morning; the God-consciousness that prays even in the middle of a heated argument, "Lord, bless my tongue!"

All of the keys to sustaining faith in these two devotions are related to, and focused on, Jesus. None is a quick-fix or a magic talisman; all depend on the presence of Christ, and on His sovereign will. In the midst of life's fragmenting stress, remember that *"In him (Christ) all things hold together"* (Col. 1:17, *NIV*). It is in the working of Him who holds even our lives together that these six keys to sustaining faith have the power to unlock every door Satan may slam in our faces. Hallelujah!

Praise in Prayer

Dear Father, help me to praise You with honesty even when I am troubled, to sing even in the darkness and to continue steadfastly in prayer. Sustain my faith, I pray through Jesus, Amen.

Selected Readings

Psalm 70	Ephesians 6:10-20
Romans 12:9-21	Philippians 4:4-7

Praise in Practice

1. Try reading Psalm 70 and substituting a problem of faith-threatening difficulty for the psalmist's enemies. Affirm God's power over them.

2. Share a situation when prayer leaped to your lips without any formality such as, "Let us pray."

47
Ripples from the Center of Praise

---

*"Blow the trumpet at the time of the New
Moon, at the full moon, on our solemn feast
day. For this is a statute for Israel, and a law
of the God of Jacob...for a testimony, when He
went throughout the land of Egypt."*
—Psalm 81:3,5

Thoughtful leaders in the Church have long perceived a
pattern in Scriptures such as this—an order of priorities
for believers. In referring to the feast of the New Moon,
the psalmist is concerned first of all about the *worship
and praise of God*. He then mentions *Israel*, the *people*
among whom the feast was established. And finally he
refers to the feast as a testimony to *unbelievers*—in this
case, the Egyptians who witnessed God's deliverance of
Israel.

This three-fold order is essential for the effective

work and witness of the Church in the world. It is a God-ordained system of stepping-stones: *worship* first, *fellowship* among God's people second, and *evangelism* third. We ignore to our peril the sequence of these ministries.

Note first that both ministry to the Body (fellowship) and ministry to the world (evangelism) are *rooted in worship and praise*. This does not stem from an insistence on God's part that unless we pay lip service to Him before we turn to others He will sulk and pout. Rather, worship and praise does two essential things *to* us before God's power can work most freely *through* us. *First,* in worship we submit ourselves to His Throne and welcome His Kingdom grace and power into our lives, individually, and into our congregation collectively. *Second,* worship grounds the worshiper on the solid foundation of the Word of God, bringing a spirituality and relationship with God that is absolutely essential to release the love and power essential for genuine fellowship and effective evangelism. Evangelism without worship as a prerequisite is like launching a mission without contacting headquarters. Before the church at Antioch dared to launch a missionary enterprise, they *fasted and prayed*; their sending of missionaries was a byproduct of worship, not a "scheme" contrived by man's understanding or zeal (Acts 13:1-3).

Worship is the beginning point, and as a rock thrown in a pond, ripples emanate outward; so from this center of praise *fellowship* proceeds. By "fellowship," I don't necessarily mean potluck suppers, though common meals can be a great boon to genuine fellowship. But the real issue at stake is that the saints themselves be united in love, open to one another, mutual sharers in all Jesus has bequeathed to His new community. This interaction develops a love which more naturally advances an effective witness to the world.

Evangelism is not the exclusive domain of the Lone-Ranger-type who launches out on his own. Effective evangelism involves the Body. Even Paul, who was as individually selected for an evangelistic mission as anyone could be, was still sent out by and remained accountable to the church at Antioch. When leaders of Christ's flock feed and lead the sheep in His life and love, evangelism will result as a natural "spillover," and the lost will be drawn to the genuineness of the life they see among the redeemed community (Acts 2:46,47). Evangelism is a sharing of the love of God. And it is best shared by people who have interacted and bonded with each other until, as in a loving marriage, what they have naturally multiplies.

Thus, worship spawns the ministry and assures the success of the task of evangelism itself. We *worship,* and see the release of His Kingdom power and presence; we *fellowship,* and see the love of God multiply in the Body; and then we *evangelize*—not by constraint, so much as by the nature of the grace that has been plunged in the pond of our church setting. The ripples of praise run out to the town, the city and to every far-flung shore. But it all starts with putting praise at the center.

Praise in Prayer

Praise and glory to You, dear God, for sending Your Son and establishing our relationship to You through Him. We rejoice in You, and anticipate sharing this grace both among ourselves and with those who need to respond to Your love. Grant us perception in seeing the divine priority in the sequencing of these ministries. Through Christ our Lord, Amen.

Selected Readings

Isaiah 49:1-6   Acts 13:42-52
Luke 24:46-53   Romans 12:9,10

Praise in Practice

1. How does Acts 1:8 reflect the order suggested in today's devotional reading? (Link Acts 1:8 with Luke 24:46-53.)

2. In what ways could your own church life strengthen each of these three emphases?

> Worship—
> Fellowship—
> Evangelism—

48

Beyond Transcendence: Caught Up to Plunge In

"The Lord is high above all nations, and His glory above the heavens. Who is like the Lord our God, who dwells on high, who humbles Himself to behold the things that are in the heavens and in the earth?"—Psalm 113:4-6

Worship and praise by definition enable the worshiper to transcend the earthly plane. The psalmist's focus on a God who is "high above" lifts Him out of discouragement and defeat, gives him a view from the mountaintop and puts earth in the perspective of heaven. This is not to say that the worshiper has been "beamed up" out of the world into an unreality, or brought to the presence of a God who cannot be bothered with mundane human existence. But, the God "high above" *is* a God who "raises the poor out of the dust, and lifts the needy out of the ash heap" (vs. 7). He helps us transcend our limits, born up from a worship that transcends the limits of our world in at least three ways.

Worship *transcends the temporal.* We want to learn to offer worship "in season, out of season"—with constancy and faithfulness instead of whimsy and fleeting feelings. It's amazing how becoming caught up in worship can make us say, "Where did the time go!"; for true worship transcends time. But it also transcends more than a sense of "time on the clock." Worship lifts us beyond the limits of those things that time and life have engrained into our systems of thought and habit. Worship works a release from the constraints that years of sin and bondage have woven and warped in us.

Worship *transcends the traditional.* Living worship is never static, but always finds fresh and vital ways of expressing praise to God Most High; otherwise, the finest worship patterns will easily degenerate into rote recitations and deadening dullness. Of course none of us lives without tradition, and it can be an *en*abler of worship rather than a *dis*abler. Yet praying for the new wine of the Spirit requires us to be ready to find the old *re*newed; wineskins stretched anew that can contain God's renewing freshness.

And true worship *transcends the theoretical.* Worship is not merely a cerebral, mystical or emotional experience. It is the humbling of the entire human being—body and mind, spirit and emotions—before the Creator-Redeemer. True worship transcends the vain supposition that human energy can "get things going," and recognizes that God is the source and ground of all our becoming, doing and accomplishing.

Again, this emphasis on worship that "transcends" must not trick us into thinking that entering the Throne room on high is a removal *from* reality. In fact, it is an entrance *into* it. Worship catches us *up* to God only to plunge us *into* and prepare us to deal *with* the most earthy issues. Transcendent worship accompanied the commissioning of the early disciples to teach all nations (Matt. 28:16-20). Transcendent worship accompanied the establishment of the Church (Acts 2:1-14). Transcendent worship equipped the Christian martyr, Stephen, to endure stoning with the prayer, "Lord, do not charge them with this sin" (Acts 7:60).

Let us never speak of the need to "make worship relevant to life." Worship *is* life. Entering the Throne room of God "on high" is an activity perfectly suited to earth-bound people; it ennobles and enables them to deal with earthly situations in His transcendent power.

Praise in Prayer

Dear Father, blot forever from my mind any notion or thinking that You dwell in a far-off, other-worldly realm, and that worshiping You is not intimately related to this world. Grant that my visits to Your Presence will only equip me to heal the hurts around me. In Jesus' name, Amen.

Selected Readings

Psalm 61   Psalm 107:23-32

Psalm 69:29-36   Isaiah 57:15-21

Praise in Practice

1. Think about and discuss the difference between *worship*, and *thinking about* and *discussing* worship.

2. When faced with a problem or crisis, what is likely to be your first reaction? To act? To think about the problem and a possible solution? To pray? When might it be appropriate to act first?

49
Altars of Worship: The Widening Light

*"Oh, send out Your light and Your truth! Let
them lead me; let them bring me to Your holy
hill and to Your tabernacle. Then I will go to
the altar of God, to God my exceeding joy."*
—Psalm 43:3,4

Long before man began to make written records of his
quest for faith, he was a worshiping being. The crude
but expressive drawings on the walls of caves occupied
by lost generations depict more than their hunt for food,
but their search for what the psalmist calls the "light" of
true worship. The Jewish Scriptures record the earliest
dealings between man and the true God. God aided
the quest by sending the light of revelation, and in His
light we find at least five types of altars—even before
the altars prescribed by the Law of Moses; altars point-
ing toward *the* altar that is Jesus Christ. Each altar is represented by a Bible figure.

Seth, the first generation from Adam and Eve, lived in a time when people groped toward a *dimly lit altar*. As a result of the Fall, death reigned (Rom. 5:14). But to the credit of Seth and the people of his day, "men began to call on the name of the Lord" (Gen. 4:26). God granted them the light of His moral law, and an introductory revelation of His nature, in disclosing His "name" or character. At this altar people could offer gifts that were pleasing or displeasing, as in the case of Cain and Abel, according to their moral choices.

Noah represents an *altar of new beginnings.* "Noah was a just man, perfect in his generations. Noah walked with God" (Gen. 6:9), and therefore he and his family were spared from the judgment of the flood. After the ark had come to rest on dry land, "Noah built an altar to the Lord," and God promised a new start for humanity (8:20-22); the worship of a God where mercy always exceeds His judgment.

Abraham represents the *altar of faith*. Wanting to demonstrate Himself more fully before a sinful world, God called Abraham to be the ancestor of a special people among whom He would reveal His will. Although he was surrounded by idols, Abraham responded to this call by sheer faith. Leaving his homeland, he "built an altar to the Lord" (Gen. 12:7). The several other altars Abraham would build testify not only to his devotion, but to his faith. Here is the worship which sees God's promise for you and its implications for the world.

Isaac stands for the *altar of fulfilled promises*. The story of faith is the story of promise and fulfillment. Isaac was the answer to God's promise that Abraham and Sarah would have a child through whom the promise would be fulfilled. Isaac proves that "second generation" believers can have a vital faith, because he, too, "built an altar...and called on the name of the Lord" (Gen. 26:25). Here is the worship that secures a new generation and lays the foundation for what will be advanced in the next generation.

Then there is *Jacob*, son of Isaac and father of the twelve tribes of Israel, and representing the *altar of expanded vision*. From a scheming, devious person, Jacob is summoned by his vision of the "ladder" extending into heaven and the renewal of the promise given first to father Abraham. An enlarged man, Jacob built an altar there, calling the place "the house of God" (Gen. 28:18-22). His more complete transformation at Peniel (Gen. 32) would follow, but the vision he receives at Bethel points to worship that summons us *to* the will of God, that later we may be changed *in* the will of God.

All biblical altars point, of course, to the ultimate sacrifice, Jesus the Christ. Each of these stands as testimony to the innate desire of man to worship, but primarily to the power in the love of a God which leads us in progressing brighter light to His "holy hill" and tabernacle—to the altar of His only Son, the ultimate Light of the world.

Praise in Prayer

O God of time, You have graced us with the privilege of living in the fullness of time, and of coming to You through the sacrifice of Jesus. We

*praise You for granting us this light and guiding
us to the true altar. We honor Jesus for His willingness to sacrifice Himself for us. In His name,
Amen.*

Selected Readings

Genesis 35:1-7   Psalm 84:1-4
Leviticus 1:1-9   Hebrews 13:10-16

Praise in Practice

1. Was the concept of an altar only for Old Covenant
believers? If Christians also have an altar, what sacrifice
is offered on it?

2. What is the main difference between the Jewish
and the Christian altars? Why does Hebrews 13:10 sound
protective about this distinction?

50

Moses, and the Blessings of Worship

"Bless the Lord, O my soul, and forget not all His benefits:...The Lord executes righteousness and justice for all who are oppressed. He made known His ways to Moses, His acts to the children of Israel."—Psalm 103:2,6,7

I've pointed several times to the fact that worship has been ordained to both spiritually and practically expand and benefit the worshiper; that it is not as though God *needed* our worship. While our Father rejoices in our love and fellowship, His greatest desire is to bless *us*. In the account of God's call to Moses, celebrated here by the psalmist, some of these transforming "benefits" of worship are demonstrated.

In the Exodus 3 account, where the angel of the Lord appears to Moses in the burning bush, God's calling of Moses' name seizes his attention. As he approaches, God warns, "Do not draw near this place. Take your sandals off your feet, for the place where you stand is holy ground" (Exod. 3:5).

Moses' first discovery is not only that God is to be reverenced, but that worship is intended to strip us of our own works (shoes) and lead us to stand alone in God's work (the earth).

Further, in this first worship encounter at Sinai, Moses' reticence and timidity will be impacted. He will move from being a man filled with excuses why he isn't fit for God's will for him, to a man ready to begin a pathway of learning and growth in God's will. In encountering God's awesome might in worship, Moses begins the journey forward. He will discover that *he*, too, will find more power than he thought—that God uses worship as an occasion to confer His own power on the worshipers. Is there a greater benefit to worship than such discoveries?

It was, of course, *in* worship that God called Moses to lead a people *from* bondage to the world system *unto* a life of worship in His divine order. He was commissioned to return to Egypt as an instrument of God's deliverance. So it is with God's summons to each of us; to come to Him, and through worship to become fashioned as an instrument of His power. What a joy to stand before the One who champions the cause of those who are unjustly imprisoned and persecuted, who are bound by the chains of illness and poverty and sin and suffering. Yes, our worship is intended to bring blessings to us, but the inevitable fruit of vital worship will be a transformed people who become transforming instruments of God's grace and deliverance to the world. As the book of Revelation reveals, all who worship the Lamb-who-is-the-Lion, will defeat the Adversary and vanquish the power of sin's dominion over others (see Rev. 17:14).

Moses' first worship encounter realized one of the most fundamental of all the blessings of worship: finding and serving the will of God. There is the essence of worship! Praising the God who made you enables you find or cease resisting His will for you, and to identify the task that is best for you in His service.

Small wonder the psalmist says, "Forget not all His benefits—BLESS THE LORD!" The next time your worship seems wearying or you find yourself preoccupied or upset, remember Moses' discoveries...and "forget not all His benefits"! You never know when your worship encounter with the Lord may become a pathway to power for the deliverance of someone else.

Praise in Prayer

Praise You, Holy Father, for knowing me better than I know myself. Bless You, Lord Jesus, for bringing divine deliverance into the world. Thank You, Holy Spirit, for helping me be open to learning how I can better cooperate with Your working in the world, as I walk in worship and let You teach me further of the Father's purpose for me. Through Jesus my Lord, Amen.

Selected References

Exodus 4:27-30   Isaiah 46:1-4
Psalm 25:4-11   John 14:12-14

Praise in Practice

1. Are you comfortable with the concept of "benefiting" from the worship of God? Do you think the principle can be abused?

2. Think about your growth since you first became a Christian. Has worshiping and serving God revealed anything to you about *yourself*?

3. Does identifying yourself with the will of God make you more aware of and sensitive to those suffering from sin, illness, injustice or oppression? To make you an instrument of deliverance?

51

Of New Tricks and Good Public Relations

"How sweet are Your words to my taste, sweeter than honey to my mouth! Through Your precepts I get understanding; therefore I hate every false way."—Psalm 119:103,104

Our praise will not be perfected until we can truly say with the psalmist that the precepts of God are as sweet as honey. Too often, I'm afraid, we have a sentimental "bent" toward God, without a full understanding of how to do things His way. The story of Uzzah is a case in point.

Uzzah was a part of King David's expedition to retrieve the Ark. As we earlier noted, God promised the Ark would be the place where His glory would dwell and David coveted that blessing, properly. But he appears at first to be unaware of God's explicit instructions about how the Ark was to be transported. It was equipped with gold rings at each corner, through which long poles were thrust; and certain priests from the tribe of Levi were to carry the Ark with these poles. But David uses a cart instead—apparently because the Philistines had done so.

Now God had not dealt kindly with the Philistines after they had previously captured the Ark from Israel. They anxiously asked the priests of the pagan god Dagon what to do, and the priests advised them to put it on a new cart and send it back into Israelite territory. The new cart may have been to curry favor with this strange God of the Israelites; but it was hardly in harmony with God's plan to have only consecrated Levites carry the Ark.

At any rate, years later when David seeks to return the Ark to Jerusalem, he sets out with a company of men. And peculiarly, just as the Philistines had, they sat the Ark atop a new cart they built for its "comeback." Can you imagine the procession? (See the story in 2 Samuel 6.) David and his aides began with song and instrumental music as they rejoiced...and here came the Ark on its cart.

A man named Ahio was in front, and his brother Uzzah was bringing up the rear, tending to the swaying cart with its precious contents. I imagine that Ahio was up front because his name means "brotherly." Like all good "front" men, he's the suave, "well met" NICE guy—the public relations man. And Uzzah—well, let's imagine him as a husky man with enough brawn to give the cart a boost from behind the cart when needed, for his name means "strength." What else would you need? Here we have a means of transportation ordained by priests, plus resourceful men in front and rear.

The answer is, however, that the "what else" we need is *obedience*. All these arrangements were foreign to God's will. *Sacrifice,* not *style,* was to precede the Ark. And it was to be *carried,* not *carted!* Tragedy struck: the oxen stumbled, and burly Uzzah put out his hand to steady it—well-meaning, perhaps—but against the God-ordained requirement that only the consecrated priests could touch the Ark. And Uzzah dropped dead!

It was a tragic lesson. We may be thankful that God doesn't deal this abruptly today, but there is a "death penalty" of lost vitality whenever we become guilty of trying to "steady our arks" in our own way, with our own PR, in our own strength, with our own plans and programs. Whether ordained by "pagan priests" or not, we're on a dead-end street when we succumb to world-patterned worship. We can never advance God's Kingdom effectively by the ways of that spirit.

Let us hear God's Word as it confronts us where such ignorance or arrogance may blind or tempt us. Let us build on the rock of His ways, walk in the light of His will, and offer our worship according to His Word.

Praise in Prayer

Lord, we praise You for the Lamp of Your Word. Help us to walk in its light instead of the traditions of men. Help our worship to be so genuine that we are glad to submit our will to Yours. In Christ's name we pray, Amen.

Selected Readings

2 Samuel 6:1-11   Matthew 15:1-9
Jeremiah 10:23,24   Romans 6:15-23

Praise in Practice

1. Read Hebrews 5:8,9. Why do you think Jesus, who was sinless, had to learn obedience?

2. Read Matthew 15:1-9. What human rule had the Pharisees substituted for the commandment of God? Why does behavior like this make our worship in vain?

52
Meet Me at the Mercy Seat

---

*"Remember, O Lord, Your tender mercies and
Your lovingkindnesses, for they have been from
of old. Do not remember the sins of my youth,
nor my transgressions; according to Your
mercy remember me, for Your goodness' sake,
O Lord."*—Psalm 25:6,7

It's appropriate to follow our reflection on God's ways
and how the Ark was handled, and look at the other
side of the coin. Even though God was meticulously
insistent on His terms—requiring obedience in how the
Ark was carried—the same Ark also served as the "seat"
of God's loving mercy and grace that our psalmist
extols here.

In addition to the tables of stone on which the Law
was engraved, the Ark had another important feature
positioned above its contents. It was an ornate lid,

which the Bible beautifully calls, "the mercy seat." Since no human could ever keep the commandments perfectly, God had a *sign of His grace* joined to the very *symbol of His law*.

The mercy seat consisted of a large "sea" or plate of pure gold, with a cherub—a mysterious winged creature we often find attending God at His throne—at both ends of the Ark. Their great wings were stretched out toward each other, covering the plate of gold. And God promised Moses that He would meet him there at the mercy seat. (See Exod. 25:17-22.)

Of course it's only at a place of mercy and grace that we can ever meet God. Careful obedience to the Word is our goal, though perhaps not our perfected accomplishment. In truth, not one of us is worthy to stand in God's presence; so, in love, He condescends to meet us at the mercy seat.

I occasionally hear people say they did not partake of the Lord's Supper at its service in their church, "Because I just didn't feel worthy." Bless your heart, dear one, no one would ever enjoy the communion meal if that were the requirement! That word "worthy," used to remind us never to partake "un-worthily" (1 Cor. 11:29), is from an ancient term referring to a coin whose gold or silver content balanced exactly with its minted worth. When the coin became old and worn, it would not balance—it would be "worth-less," i.e. worth-less-than-when-minted. It was *un*-worthy.

We are all like a used coin—not worthless in the sense of being of absolutely no value, but simply "worth less" than we were when we were "newly minted" at creation. The image of God that was stamped on us at creation has become worn, and there's nothing there sufficient to buy salvation. But Jesus comes and says reassuringly, "I'll pour my worth into you! I'll re-mint you! I'll give you new life. I'll put you back in circulation."

No, you aren't worthy to partake, and neither am I. But we meet each other at the mercy seat because it is there that we find God's tender mercies—which all of us need, and which restores worth and welcomes us "to the altar of God"—His presence, and His Table.

Praise in Prayer

God of grace, we praise You for meeting us not on the terms of the Law but at the mercy seat. Help us to show that we value the cost of free grace by responding in loving obedience. We pray through Christ our Lord, Amen.

Selected Readings

Psalm 23   Psalm 123
Psalm 103:1-14   Ephesians 2:1-10

Praise in Practice

1. Suppose a follower of a religious system that depends on works asked you to illustrate the Christian concept of grace or "unmerited favor" from everyday life. What is the best illustration or story you've heard, or can think of?

2. Discuss this definition of "cheap grace," sharing whether you agree or disagree with it: "Cheap grace is the preaching of forgiveness without requiring repentance, baptism without church discipline, communion without confession, absolution without personal confession. Cheap grace is grace without discipleship, grace without the cross, grace without Jesus Christ, living and incarnate."[1]

Note

1. Dietrich Bonhoeffer, *The Cost of Discipleship* (New York: Macmillan Publishing, 1966), p. 47.

53

The Difference Between Being Holy and Perfect

---

*"Lord, who may abide in Your tabernacle?
Who may dwell in Your holy hill? He who
walks uprightly, and works righteousness, and
speaks the truth in his heart;...he who does
these things shall never be moved."*
—Psalm 15:1,2,5

Let's look again at this text's double paradoxical problem of our call to do good works ("speaks the truth...walks uprightly,") and our human inability to walk in total perfection (our need for God's abiding grace). The resolution to the paradox is found if we can note that holiness is not so much something we do, as someone we are—in Christ, and the someone He is enabling us to become!

Being holy is not projected in God's Word as an effort we pursue so desperately we lose our sense of peace or confidence, or one that deprives our spontaneity or joy in worship. The recurring Scripture, "You shall therefore be holy, for I am holy" (as in Lev. 11:45, for example), is not mandating an achievement of sinless perfection so much as offering a marvelous, uplifting promise. Those words are not a heavy-handed commandment imposing itself from the outside of our being, but they convey God's promise that being/becoming holy is more of a family trait, a genetic characteristic that His life *in* us will manifest in time.

For example, any who know me also know that I have a receding hairline. There's a very good reason for that: my dad had a receding hairline...and his dad had one, too. But my father never said to me, as a boy, "Now Jack, when you get to be about twenty-five I want you to start losing your hair, in order to prove I'm your father." Rather, my balding progresses because it's a family trait.

The same is true of my larger-than-average nose. But again, it didn't grow because my mother pulled on it or my dad demanded it. I simply eventually "manifested" the same sort of nose my dad had, *because his life is in me.* So in the same way, the heavenly Father has said, "You *will* become holy—for I am holy and my life is in you!"

Jesus' promise is that those who come to Him will have the Father's "eternal life" (John 3:16, *NIV*). This "life" isn't eternal solely in the sense of its *quantity* of life (i.e., life unending); but it also refers to a *quality* of life, the Father's type, that is poured into the life of us who are born again.

In the days of the Ark of the Covenant, this life was symbolized by Aaron's rod that budded. It's a magnificent picture of Christ's resurrection, as our vindicated High Priest, but there's another picture there. He said, "Because I live you too shall live!", and therein is the promise of His nature in us bringing His holiness to bear on not only our sin, but on our propensity as broken sinners for continued sinning. He not only forgives, but He breaks the tendency of sin's power to rule us. And when we respond to the Father's forgiving grace and life in us, Jesus' mighty resurrection power will bring vitality to our daily walk, and we will *bud!* The "dry stick" of our limitations will blossom with God's holiness, and He will be seen in us.

Praise in Prayer

I praise You, Father, for Your majestic holiness. Even when my actions are less than holy, I look to Your holiness and long to be more like You. I praise You for the cleansing blood of Christ which makes me whole; and for Your nature transmitted to me through Jesus' resurrection power. Help me to respond by drawing on that power to be holy in Your sight. In Jesus Name, Amen.

Selected Readings

Isaiah 62:10   1 Corinthians 3:16,17
Romans 8:1-11   1 Peter 1:13-21

Praise in Practice

1. Free association: What picture first comes to mind when you think of the idea of being "holy"? Is it a picture informed by the Bible or by tradition?

2. Sometimes it's more helpful to dwell on the holiness of God instead of on the Christian obligation to be holy. What clue to why this is true is given in 1 Samuel 2:2?

3. In a Bible dictionary, look up the words "holy" and "sanctified." Do these concepts refer more to a state into which God places believers, or to sinless perfection?

54

Foreign Gods and Profane Fire

*"There shall be no foreign god among
you;...But my people would not heed My voice,
and Israel would have none of Me. So I gave
them over to their own stubborn heart, to walk
in their own counsels."*—Psalm 81:9,11,12

They were priests, sons of Aaron, and should have
known to "heed God's voice," as the psalmist puts it.
Nadab and Abihu knew how to offer sacrifice in the
way God prescribed. But this time they thought they
had a better idea. They took the censers which should
have been filled with God-ordained fire to ignite the
sacrifices, and filled them instead with "profane
fire...which He had not commanded them" (Lev. 10:1).
And they died.

"Profane" means *before* or *outside the temple*. In the
Old Testament context it is action that is outside the

boundaries set by the holy God. The story of Nadab and Abihu illustrates the psalmist's point that the way we worship *counts*. We can worship in God's way, or we can go our own way. That amounts to self-worship; and since "self" without God is not eternal or durable, the inevitable end of such people is "self" destruction. Sadly, Bible history is punctuated with other similar cases.

Cain went his own way in worship. We are not given many specifics, though it seems God had ordained an animal sacrifice such as Abel offered. But Cain, being a tiller of the ground, thought that something from his farm plot would do (see Gen. 4:1-5). At any rate, when God honored Abel's offering, Cain was jealous, and we find the sad but familiar story of the world's first murder. From profane or unauthorized worship to murder? The link isn't as obscure as we might think. Refusing to worship God's way is self-destructive, and it's but a short step from there to being destructive toward others.

The people who built the tower of Babel ignored God's way in favor of their own. Instead of honoring God, they said, "Let us make a name for *ourselves*" (Gen. 11:4; emphasis mine). And just as the psalmist said, God gave them over to the stubbornness of their heart and scattered them abroad. Profane plans—schemes laid "outside the temple"—just won't work out in the long run.

The Israelites who built the golden calf were guilty of profane worship. In their case, it was all too clear that they were not just calf worshipers but "will-worshipers," too, because in its presence they did what they wished—they "sat down to eat and drink, and rose up to play" (Exod. 32:6). Here is an instance where literally "Israel would have none of me"; so God gave them up, and struck them down.

Such instances do not depict a capricious or vindictive God who destroys people for thinking for themselves. They merely describe the end of stubborn, willful worship. It is self-destructive; and if that's what we want, God gives us over to it.

A happier picture emerges when people remember the basic meaning of worship in the first place. It is to bow, to attribute worth to, to obey, to honor, *another*—God—not ourselves. It is not the way of Nadab and Abihu, or of Cain and the people at Babel and the calf-worshipers among Israel. It is the way of Abraham, Isaac and Jacob, of Moses and the prophets. It is above all the way of Jesus Himself, who said, "Not my will but thine be done."

Praise in Prayer

We honor You alone as the one true God, Dear Father. Yet we confess that our own will can easily contest Your supreme position as Lord of our lives. Help my worship to be ordered after what pleases You, rather than what tickles our own fancy. Through Him who submitted His own will to Yours, Amen.

Selected Readings

Psalm 40:4-8   Isaiah 31:1-3
Psalm 143:7-10   Isaiah 46

Praise in Practice

1. How can we be sure that the way we worship is pleasing to God, instead of consisting of forms that we have devised out of our own will?

2. How would you defend the justice of God to someone who objects that Nadab and Abihu suffered unjust punishment at His hands?

3. How can *self-denial* even be a form of self-centered worship? (See Colossians 2:18-23.)

55

The Kind of Worship God Blesses

"Behold, how good and how pleasant it is for brethren to dwell together in unity!...It is like the dew of Hermon, descending upon the mountains of Zion; for there the Lord commanded the blessing—life forevermore."
—Psalm 133:1,3

"That service really blessed me!"

It's good to hear responses like that after a gathering for public worship. Often it's the result of the free flow of the Spirit, symbolized in the Scriptures as an "anointing"—like that referred to in this psalm. Moving music ministry, testimonies or healthy Bible teaching are also "anointed," but in Psalm 133, it's especially *corporate unity* that receives the "anointing" and God's appointed blessing. Have we given sufficient attention to the unity of the Body as a key proviso—as an avenue through which God has chosen to bless His people?

Now, we may have to use our imagination some to appreciate the imagery of this psalm. To say that unity is as pleasant as oil running down Aaron's head on to his beard and garments (vs. 2) may sound a little strange to us. But if you've ever been involved in a congregation torn apart by division, you can easily make the connection between the blessing of church harmony and the refreshment of early morning dew atop a mountain in a hot Mediterranean climate.

As churches of today move into worship renewal it's not uncommon for them to experience some struggle and strain. Old traditions may be disrupted. Understanding about what worship leaders are attempting may be slow in coming. Although each fellowship must work through these issues in its own way, I've found five elements to be usually present when the Body successfully negotiates the waters of renewal.

There is first of all a general *willingness* for the worship to be rescued from spirit-deadening routine to Spirit-led vitality. Unfortunately, like taking medicine, it's sometimes necessary for us to hurt before we want to change; and people who see nothing wrong with worship as it always has been may not hurt enough to be willing to change.

Sensitivity must characterize a substantial number of people and worship leaders for unified worship renewal. They must have an instinct for what God wants, and for what best enables people to render publicly what they feel for God in their hearts.

There must be widespread *understanding* if the Body is to move forward together in worship. Here the responsibility of teachers and preachers cannot be over-emphasized. God's people will generally respond positively to changes that are shown to be grounded in the Word and will of God.

The leaders must have a certain *alertness* to congregational reaction, especially if innovations in worship are attempted. This doesn't mean that pastors are to be lackeys moving only according to the whim of the majority. It does mean that they are ministers to *the Body*, not just ministers of God. If they are disinterested or blind to whether what happens in worship is really accomplishing renewal, unified worship is impossible.

And let's face it: There must be a certain level of *ability* on the part of worship leaders if the Body responds in unity. This is not an appeal for slick and skillful techniques. It is an appeal for offering our best in worship. God was not pleased when His Old Covenant people offered sacrifices of blemished animals. And neither He nor His New Covenant people respond favorably to sloppy and careless worship leadership today.

Are you doing your part to make the corporate worship of the Body so pleasantly unified that it's a true *anointing?*

Praise in Prayer

We praise You, Father, Son and Holy Spirit, for the unity You manifest. We repent of the disunity manifested among Your people, and we pray for a renewed willingness to accept the

unity of the Spirit in the bond of peace. Through
Christ we pray, Amen.

Selected Readings

Romans 15:1-7   1 Corinthians 11:17-34
1 Corinthians 1:10-17 Ephesians 4:1-16

Praise in Practice

1. In Romans 15:5,6, what specific *result* of a spirit of
unity is anticipated?

2. Suppose you are a part of a church with a wide
variety of personal tastes and preferences in worship
styles. Make a list of the factors that would be required
to keep the Body unified during a time of worship
renewal.

56
Understanding the Heart of God

---

*"He heals the broken-hearted and binds up
their wounds. He counts the number of the
stars; He calls them all by name. Great is our
Lord, and mighty in power; His understanding
is infinite. The Lord lifts up the humble."*
—Psalm 147:3-6

How grand to praise a God whose vast understanding
encompasses the names of the stars, *and* whose
detailed attentiveness in love knows each individual
heart and need as well! How magnificently this text
asserts the grandeur of God's love—how it reveals His
heart to "lift up" the sinful and not to "put us down."

This knowledge was made clearest to us all when
Jesus came and rearranged mankind's view of God.
Jesus repeatedly told parables, stories that countered
man's confused picture of the Father. In three of these,

Jesus dealt with the human inclination to focus more on our guilt than on God's grace: the stories of the lost *sheep,* the lost *coin* and the lost *son*—all recorded in Luke 15.

The parable of the lost sheep (Luke 15:1-7) reveals that in the heart of God *no one is unimportant.* God is never so preoccupied with "safe" (saved) people that He is not concerned about the one person at risk. God *counts* His sheep. If He has a flock of a hundred, and notices that only ninety-nine trot into the fold at night, He doesn't say, "Too bad—one scoundrel is missing!" Rather, He goes into the night, goes into the wilderness, goes to find that one solitary lamb, and putting it on His shoulders He returns home rejoicing.

Whatever guilt or aloneness we may feel, look, listen and praise God that you are a precious sheep this valuable in His eyes!

The parable of the lost coin (vss. 8-10) shows God's glad anticipation of being reunited in a working partnership with us. The reason for this woman's eagerness to find the lost silver coin is that it was on the order of an engagement ring—part of a set of *ten* coins woven together and worn as a necklace at her wedding. But often, shamed by our sin, we may run or hide from God, oblivious not only to His *love,* but unaware that He sees us as desirable, as "needed to complete a set." He has plans for partnership with us, plans that will be crippled without us. Whatever our shame sense of unworthiness, hear how much you are desired and valued by the Father's heart.

Then, the familiar parable of the lost son (vv. 11-24),

which shows God's plans for the *complete restoration* of the lost. This glimpse into God's heart reveals a father's *waiting* for the son's return. There is no requirement for the prodigal boy to grovel at the father's feet; there is no grudging, half-way acceptance of the son's approach—no holding him at arm's length to see "if he really means it." Instead, there is a warm, glad and immediate embrace, the presentation of the best robe, the gift of a gold ring and sandals, and a jubilant welcome-home party. However distant you may feel or have been, believe this: the Father will welcome you home—gladly!

We can easily imagine that David was the author of Psalm 147. There are the references to Jerusalem, the city David loved, and to the harp, which David played. Most significant, however, is the fact that David himself had been a wandering sheep who discovered God would not abandon him; a lost coin God longed to recover to full partnership; and a prodigal son whom the father joyously welcomed home to full restoration in the family.

Many of us can bear personal testimony to having discovered these traits of the infinitely gracious heart of God. Not only is it such a wonderful revelation that we praise Him for His love; it's also true that the more we praise Him the more in-depth our understanding of His heart becomes—and the better equipped we are to relate these things to others by our words, our love and our acceptance of them.

Praise in Prayer

Praise to You, dear Father, for valuing me in spite of my sin. Help me to rely on and respond fully to the richness of Your love that I never hide in my poverty from You, but accept the wealth of Your wholehearted acceptance of me. Through Jesus I pray, Amen.

Selected Readings

Luke 15:1-7   Luke 15:11-24
Luke 15:8-10   Luke 15:25-32

Praise in Practice

1. In your experience, does God's family, the Church, typically respond to returning prodigals more as the father did, or as the elder brother?

2. Do shame and embarrassment often keep the guilty from returning to God?

57

You Can Sleep Because God Doesn't

*"I will both lie down in peace, and sleep;
for You alone, O Lord, make me dwell in
safety."*—Psalm 4:8

The Lord often awakens me during the night. Someone may suspect that it's indigestion or worry; but I've learned to tell the difference between times of sleeplessness and those when the Lord "calls," wanting to impress something on my mind. Not long ago I was awakened in this way, and went to the place in our living room where I usually go for my devotions. I wondered what it was He wanted to say to me.

I had been unusually laden with duty, much on my mind, and I shouldn't have been surprised, but it was so tender a message; simply, "Everything's going to be all right. Now, back to bed and sleep." And I did just that. Even though no *conscious* turmoil awakened me, a full plate of duty was introducing a mental "indigestion" that needed the Father's assuring word of comfort— mostly, the comfort of His personal interest and promise of provision.

The psalmist says, "He who keeps you will not slumber. Behold, He who keeps Israel shall neither slumber nor sleep" (121:3,4). It's a part of the supernatural nature of God that He isn't subject to the weariness of body and spirit that makes sleep essential for human beings. One is reminded of the simple words reportedly spoken by Pope John XXIII upon retiring nightly: "I go to sleep, Lord. The Church is Yours."

It's hard to imagine, but apparently when we are ultimately ushered into God's divine presence in heaven, we won't need sleep, either. At least John's report of his vision of the New Jerusalem states, "And there shall be no night there: They need no lamp nor light of the sun, for the Lord God gives them light" (Rev. 22:5). If we sleep in heaven we'll apparently have to learn to do it in the daytime!

But in any case, in this life we *do* need our sleep. Worry and depression and life's oft-hectic pace can make this a problem. Car trouble, a business reversal, a problem in personal or family relationships, difficulty on the job—any of a thousand other things—can interfere with our sleep. Like a thief, sleeplessness can creep into our minds under cover of night's dark shades, and rob us of the sleep we need.

When it happens, declare this firm promise! It's ours, from the Creator of night and day, who promises we can both lie down in peace, and sleep. Make your last thought at night that God is up, is well, and is remaining watchful over you and all that concerns you. Leave things to Him. He can get more done on your problem while you're asleep than you can awake!

Praise in Prayer

You created me to sleep, dear Lord, and You know how much I need. As I need rest, rest my soul in the assurance of Your constant care and watchfulness. And when I need to be awake, open my eyes and ears—alert me to Your voice and Your will. I trust myself to You, O Father; the Lord of both my nights and my days, Amen.

Selected Readings

1 Kings 18:20-29   Ecclesiastes 8:16,17
Proverbs 3:19-26; 6:20-22   Jeremiah 31:23-26

Praise in Practice

1. Do your sleeping habits reflect worry? Depression? What do you do during times when you can't sleep? Share with others any measures you've found to help.

2. Write up a little scene describing a situation that is similar to the fact that God doesn't sleep, but is in charge of the world even through the darkest night...situations that illustrate His care for you. For example, imagine that you're a king, and you have a trusted

guard posted at the castle door. Be creative as you write this brief scene. Read this "bedtime story" to yourself just before going to bed at night.

3. Do some people sleep too much? Have you known this to happen to you, or to someone you love? (See Proverbs 6:1-5,6-11).

58

I Want Somebody to Know My Name

"O Lord, You have searched me and known me. You know my sitting down and my rising up; You understand my thought afar off. You comprehend my path and my lying down, and are acquainted with all my ways."
—Psalm 139:1-3

Cathy Meeks was a young Afro-American engaged in the struggle during the racial unrest of the 1960s. She was raised a Christian and she sought to respect authority, so she was at first hesitant to take to the streets to demonstrate against injustice. But with the shooting of a black child in the Los Angeles suburb of Watts, something broke, and she felt the circumstance demanded she join the protest—so Cathy marched.

However, Cathy still felt she was caught between surging waves of humanity. On the one hand there were the defenders of the status quo, which she knew were not as just as they should be. On the other hand, she often sensed a rebellious spirit, which she felt wasn't in harmony with her Christian upbringing. She asked herself where she belonged, a question that raised deeper questions of who she was, down deep, and whether anyone really cared. Out of her agony, Cathy Meeks wrote the moving book of her experiences, titled, *I Want Somebody to Know My Name.*

Do you ever feel the same longing? Especially when torn between issues, and you wonder where God is? At such times, we all need the reassurance that we aren't "lost in space," drifting among the stars, alone and unknown in the cosmos. And that's exactly what this text addresses so eloquently. Praise the Lord, David declares this inspired statement offering just that kind of reassurance. In Psalm 139, he affirms how surely our God is not merely an impersonal force woven into a mechanical universe. The Lord is seen in such close touch with us that He is acquainted with all our ways. He is not only the God of John 3:16 who loves *the world,* He is the God of Galatians 2:20, "who loved *me* and gave Himself for *me."*

What a matter for praise! Here is the Eternal God whose almighty Word keeps spinning galaxies and worlds from falling out of orbit as they continue their trek through the vastness of space; yet He tended to my intra-uterine development (Ps. 139:13-16), and knows the number of the hairs on my head (Matt. 10:30). The God who overrules the governments of the world, and who limits the boundaries of the seas, has stooped to be my personal Shepherd (Ps. 23). He tracks the path of every soul ever born and He knows me—you—each one of His countless sheep, *by name* (John 10:3).

The desire to be known is more than a shallow quest for notoriety, like seekers lusting to see their names in lights or headlines. Rather, this quest is welcomed by our Father who calls us to Himself. Let your desire—indeed, hunger—for One to "know my name," drive you to worship at the feet of the God who not only knows you well, but who *loves* you, and wonder of wonders, who welcomes us to know Him, as well!

Praise in Prayer

I worship You, O my God, as Sovereign over the vastness of the universe, who alone has the whole world in His hand. I praise You also as my personal Lord, who knows me by name, even better than I know myself. Thank You for Your nearness and Your unfailing love for me— personally. In the name of Jesus my Lord, Amen.

Selected Readings

1 Samuel 3:1-9	Psalm 142
Psalm 8	Luke 12:6-8

Praise in Practice

1. Take a flashlight and a Bible outdoors at night— preferably when the stars are out, and in a quiet place.

Stand quietly for a few moments looking up at the sky. Breathe deeply. Try to imagine how far you're looking...and the vastness of the universe. Now use your flashlight to find and read 1 Kings 19:11-13. Apply to yourself God's question to Elijah: "What are you doing here?" Is it difficult to imagine that in all this vastness God sees you, and knows you?

2. Discuss with friends any feelings of loneliness you may have, or feelings that no one really knows the real you.

59

Walking Within My House

"I will sing of mercy and justice; to You, O Lord, I will sing praises. I will behave wisely in a perfect way....I will walk within my house with a perfect heart."—Psalm 101:1,2

How desperately the Lord seeks and our land needs homes in which people "behave wisely" today! While we may not arrive at *perfection,* we certainly can affirm our *direction* toward sinlessness and away from sin. We *can* be completely committed to making our homes places of mercy and justice—places where God is pleased to dwell.

How urgently does the Lord seek heads of families who will join with Joshua in saying, "As for me and my house, we will serve the Lord" (Josh. 24:15). Someone has worded it this way: "If the home fires are burning for God, the heart-fires will never chill."

One reason God places such importance on the family is that it is there we reveal most clearly who we really are, and who we really serve. How would I fare today if God took a census of my home—of yours—to reveal...

The way I speak and act in private;

The reading material I surround myself with;

The music that fills my dwelling;

The table talk the family shares...or doesn't;

The forgiveness displayed to one another;

The food and beverages that characterize my life-style;

The money-plans I have and exercise;

The magazines that fill the rack;

The moods I invite or tolerate;

The entertainment I seek and foster;

The media input I welcome via TV, radio, records;

The Savior I praise and worship...?

The purpose of walking through this list is neither a rigid review nor an exercise in nosiness. The fact is, God *does* take such a census. The question should really be, *What if He published it?* The bottom line is that our behavior at home indicates *whom* I am serving—Him, myself—or worse, the world system.

The call of God is to "behave wisely" at home, saying, "As for me and *everything in and about my house*, the *Lord will be served*. Not myself, not carnal entertainment, not fickle moods, not warring relationships, but Christ will be central, worshiped and glorified!"

Joshua made this application to the family by *the*

attention he gave to monuments and memorials. When God accomplished a significant victory through the people, they erected a memorial—both to honor God and to remind their children of how God worked among them.

Let's never substitute the value of Sunday School or Christian schools for the responsibility we have ourselves to our children, for we too *must* establish "memorable" and "monumental" moments. Children remember best what they see put into action. They need parents who are living "incarnations" of the Word the parents want their children to learn. Joshua's monuments demonstrate the dramatic importance of parents telling a child *how God's truth worked in their own experience.*

Take time to pour yourself into your children. Tell them how you were saved, how God has led and protected you, how He continues to lead you toward the Promised Land. There is no wiser way to "walk" within your house!

Praise in Prayer

We praise You, God, for being our Father, and for the blessings of being in Your family. Help us to live together in families of both biological and spiritual kinship in ways that glorify You. Help our private walk to indicate to those closest to us that You are our Father. Through Christ we pray, Amen.

Selected Readings

Exodus 12:21-28   Psalm 127
Joshua 4:1-7   Ephesians 6:1-4

Praise in Practice

1. Share with a group any family traditions that are like the memorials of Joshua—ways of bringing to mind the good things God has done.

2. Discuss any stresses in family life that challenge attempts to place Christ at the center. For example, have you been able to have family devotionals? Do society's demands (school, peer pressure, etc.) make it more difficult?

60

His Kingdom Is Now!

*"Your saints shall bless You. They shall speak of
the glory of Your kingdom, and talk of Your
power, to make known to the sons of men His
mighty acts, and the glorious majesty of His
kingdom."*—Psalm 145:10-12

The kingdom of Israel was never more powerful than
under David, the psalmist-king. I am not thinking primarily of David's skill as a military strategist, or of the
geographical expansion of its borders. Israel was great
under David because David was a man after God's own
heart. He endeavored to make his earthly throne a
reflection of God's eternal Kingdom, and to lead his
people in praise for its majesty.

Sometimes we long so fervently for the coming of
the Kingdom at the last great day, we forget that the
Kingdom of God, in power and glory is available *now*
to those who worship His Majesty, Jesus Christ. Our
Savior ascended the throne as the majestic Son of David
when He was raised from the dead (Acts 2:30). He com-

missioned His followers to make disciples among the nations by the authority and power of that throne (Matt. 28:18-20). The apostle Paul said that those who had responded to this invitation had been "translated...into the kingdom of the Son of His love" (Col. 1:13). His Kingdom is *now!*

This is to take nothing away from the fact that the Kingdom will not be realized in its fullness until Jesus returns in clouds of glory. But it is to impress upon us the glorious fact that we have access *now*, by faith, to the power of the King if we live and worship as citizens of His Kingdom. One of Satan's most insidious tactics is to make us look with dismay at the smaller battles he wins around us every day, forgetting that our King has already won the greatest battle; that the final revelation of His victory only awaits His chosen moment. Regardless of how bleak the circumstances may seem, or how shadowed the horizons may appear by reason of the Adversary's desperate and despicable tactics, Jesus has bequeathed to us a life of power and of triumph in the resources of His Kingdom. *Everything God has promised to be already exists. All that remains for me to do is walk with Him until we come to the place where each fulfilled promise is waiting.*

So as we walk and wait, let us worship His Majesty:

Majesty, Worship His Majesty,
Unto Jesus be all glory, honor and praise.
Majesty, Kingdom authority,
Flows from His Throne unto His own,

His anthem raise.
So exalt, lift up on high
the Name of Jesus.
Magnify, come glorify,
Christ Jesus the King.
Majesty, worship His Majesty,
Jesus who died, now glorified,
King of all kings.[1]

Praise in Prayer

King of kings, and Lord of lords, I praise you in Your majesty, acknowledging Your power over all evil and doubt and fear that would rob me of victory. In Your name, and by Your authority, I pronounce Satan and his forces to be vanquished. I bow before You, my Lord and King, and glorify the Father, by the power of Your Spirit, according to Your Word, and in Your matchless Name! Amen.

Selected Readings

Luke 11:20-22   2 Peter 1:5-11
1 Thessalonians 2:10-12 Revelation 5:8-14

Praise in Practice

1. Think about, and share if you wish, specific problems or fears in your life. When you have them clearly

in focus, ask yourself how you could confront each one with the authority given you by Jesus as a citizen in His Kingdom, with access to His power.

2. If you have access to or know by heart the music to "Worship His Majesty," above, close your praise time with this song.

Note:
1. Lyrics by Jack Hayford, © 1981 Rocksmith Music. All rights reserved.

APPENDIX

Suggestions for Your Daily Devotions

Are you looking for a simple yet effective way to invite God into your life? Many people feel this need, but have difficulty moving from a vague feeling to taking concrete steps upward to the Throne and into His Presence. Here are a few suggestions.

For private devotions, and in some family settings, there's nothing like asking God first thing in the morning to order your day. As the psalmist said, "My voice You shall hear in the morning, O Lord; in the morning I will direct it to You" (Ps. 5:3). You know we don't call it "daybreak" for nothing; for in God's presence the day can be...

- Broken open like a *gift*, surprising our hearts with His provision.
- Broken open like *an egg*, with life bursting forth as simply and brightly as a yellow chick.

- Broken open like *the sky*, with shafts of light splitting dewdrops into rainbows of promise.

Every day there are new worlds to be won through the newness that happens when we begin the day by walking with Jesus, making our steps fit into His,
in prayer,
in the Word, and
in faithful response to His love.

Whether it's at daybreak or day's end, over that mid-morning cup of coffee with a Christian neighbor or friend, at the office during the noon break, in a group or privately, here is a pattern of devotion that has been helpful to many.

1. Begin with *thanksgiving* and *praise*, simply verbalizing to God how you experience His majesty. Like aerobics, this heart-expanding experience will increase your capacity to receive more and more of Him every day.
2. Move into *confession*. Dare to name your shortcomings, facing them down in the holy name of Jesus. But don't wallow in them as though you didn't trust the blood that cleanses us from all sin! Instead, joyfully accept the forgiveness Christ offers.
3. Here you might have a *Bible reading* and/or a brief reading such as those in this book. Allow the Word to set a theme and tone to remember. If there is time, and you are in a group, focus

your awareness of the theme with discussions and exercises such as the "Praise in Practice" sections in this book.

4. *Intercede* for family, friends, church, community, nations and their leaders. Pray in specifics, trusting that the fervent prayer of righteous people "avails much" (Jas. 5:16).

5. *Submit* to the Father in prayer. It's good to kneel or raise your hands if possible, to allow your body to approve what your spirit is pledging: your willingness to live in obedience to His loving but kingly rule. A brief closing prayer is also provided in this book's readings.

I do pray that the Scriptures, the comments, and prayers in this book will open for you new and fresh vistas on the power of praise. May the time you spend with this material glorify God through His Son, and enrich your everyday walk.

Note

These suggestions are adapted from *Daybreak* by Jack Hayford (Wheaton, IL: Tyndale House, 1987).